DATE DUE

Consumer Credit Finance Charges:
Rate Information and Quotation

NATIONAL BUREAU OF ECONOMIC RESEARCH

Studies in Consumer Instalment Financing

CONSUMER CREDIT
FINANCE CHARGES
Rate Information and Quotation

WALLACE P. MORS
BABSON INSTITUTE

 1 9 6 5

NATIONAL BUREAU OF ECONOMIC RESEARCH, New York

DISTRIBUTED BY

COLUMBIA UNIVERSITY PRESS, New York and London

RELATION OF THE DIRECTORS TO THE WORK AND PUBLICATIONS OF THE NATIONAL BUREAU OF ECONOMIC RESEARCH

1. The object of the National Bureau of Economic Research is to ascertain and to present to the public important economic facts and their interpretation in a scientific and impartial manner. The Board of Directors is charged with the responsibility of ensuring that the work of the National Bureau is carried on in strict conformity with this object.

2. To this end the Board of Directors shall appoint one or more Directors of Research.

3. The Director or Directors of Research shall submit to the members of the Board, or to its Executive Committee, for their formal adoption, all specific proposals concerning researches to be instituted.

4. No report shall be published until the Director or Directors of Research shall have submitted to the Board a summary drawing attention to the character of the data and their utilization in the report, the nature and treatment of the problems involved, the main conclusions, and such other information as in their opinion would serve to determine the suitability of the report for publication in accordance with the principles of the National Bureau.

5. A copy of any manuscript proposed for publication shall also be submitted to each member of the Board. For each manuscript to be so submitted a special committee shall be appointed by the President, or at his designation by the Executive Director, consisting of three Directors selected as nearly as may be one from each general division of the Board. The names of the special manuscript committee shall be stated to each Director when the summary and report described in paragraph (4) are sent to him. It shall be the duty of each member of the committee to read the manuscript. If each member of the special committee signifies his approval within thirty days, the manuscript may be published. If each member of the special committee has not signified his approval within thirty days of the transmittal of the report and manuscript, the Director of Research shall then notify each member of the Board, requesting approval or disapproval of publication, and thirty additional days shall be granted for this purpose. The manuscript shall then not be published unless at least a majority of the entire Board and a two-thirds majority of those members of the Board who shall have voted on the proposal within the time fixed for the receipt of votes on the publication proposed shall have approved.

6. No manuscript may be published, though approved by each member of the special committee, until forty-five days have elapsed from the transmittal of the summary and report. The interval is allowed for the receipt of any memorandum of dissent or reservation, together with a brief statement of his reasons, that any member may wish to express; and such memorandum of dissent or reservation shall be published with the manuscript if he so desires. Publication does not, however, imply that each member of the Board has read the manuscript, or that either members of the Board in general, or of the special committee, have passed upon its validity in every detail.

7. A copy of this resolution shall, unless otherwise determined by the Board, be printed in each copy of every National Bureau book.

(Resolution adopted October 25, 1926,
as revised February 6, 1933, and February 24, 1941)

Contents

Contents

Tables

Tables

Charts

Acknowledgments

I AM PARTICULARLY INDEBTED to Robert P. Shay, Director of the Consumer Credit Study, who made many valuable contributions at every step of the way. Geoffrey H. Moore and F. Thomas Juster of the National Bureau and John M. Chapman of Columbia University also worked closely with me throughout the study.

Members of the Advisory Committee for the Consumer Credit Study are Paul W. McCracken, Chairman, University of Michigan; Frank Barsalou, Pacific Finance Corporation; Dorothy S. Brady, University of Pennsylvania; E. Douglas Campbell, Associates Investment Company; John M. Chapman, Columbia University; Mona Dingle, Division of Research and Statistics, Board of Governors of the Federal Reserve System; Bertrand Fox, Harvard University; Raymond W. Goldsmith, Yale University; Robert E. Lewis, First National City Bank of New York; Roger F. Murray, Columbia University and the National Bureau of Economic Research; Roland I. Robinson, Michigan State University; Herbert Stein, Committee for Economic Development; Van Buren Thorne, Jr., General Motors Acceptance Corporation; William L. Wilson, C.I.T. Financial Corporation. Others who formerly served on the Advisory Committee are Willcox B. Adsit, Gordon E. Areen, George Dimmler, the late George W. Omacht, Sidney E. Rolfe, and LeRoy A. Weller. The members of the advisory committee have generously assisted in planning and reviewing the work of the staff of the Consumer Credit Study, but their concurrence with the views expressed in this report is not to be assumed.

I wish to thank the directors' reading committee for their comments on the manuscript: Gabriel Hauge, Boris Shishkin, and Willis J. Winn. A staff reading committee of the National Bureau offered helpful comments on a draft of the study. Members were Daniel M. Holland, Massachusetts Institute of Technology; Richard M. Easterlin, University of Pennsylvania; and Roger F. Murray, Columbia University. Valuable comments also were received from Robert W. Johnson M. R. Neifeld, LeRoy A. Weller, and William L. Wilson.

Florence Liang gave statistical assistance, H. Irving Forman drew the charts, and editorial assistance was provided by Marie-Christine Culbert.

Foreword

EARLY IN THE TWENTIETH CENTURY the form in which finance charges were to be disclosed became an important part of the discussions which led to the formulation of the Uniform Small-Loan Law, first drafted in 1916 by the Russell Sage Foundation. This period witnessed the development of the modern techniques of instalment selling of durable consumer goods and the growth of the institutions which today provide a wide variety of credit services to consumers under quite different systems of computing and quoting finance charges. This study by Wallace P. Mors traces the origins of the procedures currently in use, in order to show why the consumer is faced with varying forms of information. The author goes on to analyze and evaluate the usefulness of this information to consumer borrowers.

In drawing up plans for the National Bureau's current study of consumer credit, of which this report forms a part, the subject of consumer credit finance charges was given central importance for several reasons. First, there were no statistical series measuring changes in the cost of credit, although estimates of the amount of credit extended, repaid, and outstanding had been developed in earlier National Bureau studies and later extended by Federal Reserve System estimates. Second, there had been recurrent questions about the amount of consumer credit charges in relation to the costs of providing credit. It was known that consumer credit charges were higher than those in other sectors where the amounts involved were larger and the costs consequently lower. But without empirical measurement of the relation between consumer credit charges and their component costs, there was little basis for judging whether charges were excessive or not. Third, little was known about how borrowers reacted to finance charges, and it was believed by many that lack of knowledge contributed to excessive charges and misuse of credit. Finally, there was the question of how different methods of quoting finance charges affected the ways in which borrowers used consumer credit.

The results of some studies designed to remedy these gaps in knowledge about finance charges have already appeared as National Bureau studies, and the remainder are nearing completion. The preliminary results of my work on automobile finance charges appeared as *New-Automobile Finance Rates, 1924–62*. Paul F. Smith's book, *Consumer Credit Costs, 1949–59*, revealed the relation of finance charges to component costs for four major types of credit institutions. *Consumer Sensitivity to Finance Rates*, by F. Thomas Juster and myself, showed that some borrowers are sensitive to changes in the rate of charge for credit, although relatively few estimate finance rates reasonably well. Finally, Mors's study provides a thorough analysis of the kinds of finance charge information given borrowers and its usefulness in helping to make rational credit decisions.

A major finding about the usefulness of finance charge information is that no one method of quoting charges conveys enough information about credit cost to satisfy all questions involved in credit decisions. Dollar charges, monthly or annual effective rates, and monthly payments convey valuable information, but the usefulness of each of these methods varies with different borrowing situations. As a further complication, Mors finds that state legislation contributes to a still greater diversity in information provided. He concludes that consumers do not receive easily comparable information from alternative suppliers of credit.

Mors' unraveling of the complexities in finance charge information—based on alternative mathematical formulas, legal and legislative factors, and a wide variety of credit transactions—should prove invaluable to those who seek to improve their ability to compare credit costs as well as to others who wish to evaluate the varied legislative proposals designed to expand or simplify the information given consumer borrowers.

The Consumer Credit Study was made possible by research grants to the National Bureau from four finance companies: Associates Investment Company, C.I.T. Financial Corporation, General Motors Acceptance Corporation, and Pacific Finance Corporation. These institutions are, of course, not to be held responsible for any of the statments made or views expressed in this study.

ROBERT P. SHAY
Director, Consumer Credit Study

Consumer Credit Finance Charges:

Rate Information and Quotation

1. Summary of Findings

THE USE OF CONSUMER CREDIT has grown markedly over the past half century, and particularly in recent decades. Accompanying this growth has been increasing interest in consumer credit problems. This study is concerned with one of these problems, i.e., providing finance charge (credit price) information to consumers.

It describes the methods which financing agencies and sellers use in computing finance charges and in quoting these charges to consumers; assesses the uses of the various types of finance charge information now available to consumers; discusses procedures and problems in converting various types of finance charge information to any given form; and reviews existing empirical evidence on the extent of consumer knowledge of finance charges in dollars, as computational rates and as effective annual rates.

The major conclusions are the following.

1. Three general methods of computing finance charges grew out of the varied arrangements which financing agencies and sellers constructed to provide credit to consumers under charges which, if construed as interest, were substantially above ceiling rates permissible under usury laws:

   a. Per cent per month method—developed before World War I under special (mainly remedial, credit union, and small-loan) laws exempting specified instalment cash loans from the usury laws.

   b. Discount method—developed just before World War I under a combined legal loan-hypothecated savings account repayment system which was generally upheld by courts as not usurious; later written in a more direct and simplified form as industrial loan laws (governing cash lending by industrial banks) and instalment loan laws (governing consumer cash lending by commercial banks).

    c. Add-on method—developed under the common-law time-price doctrine which makes it legally permissible for a seller to have a "cash price" and a "time price" for a good or service, the differential between the two prices not being considered interest subject to usury. The credit charge was "added on" to the cash price to obtain a time price which was to be re-paid under the terms of the credit contract.

2. Disclosure of finance charge information to borrowers varies depending on the legislative requirements and voluntary prac-tices of financing agencies and sellers. Of the various types of consumer financing laws, only small-loan laws and retail in-stalment financing laws have disclosure requirements. Small-loan laws generally require consumer finance (small-loan) com-panies to disclose rates of charge to borrowers, usually in the form of per cent per month rates. Retail instalment financing laws, enacted by most states since 1935, normally require sellers to disclose to buyers the finance charge in dollars.

3. Financing agencies and sellers vary in their voluntary disclosure of finance charges to borrowers, either in dollars or as rates of charge. Court decisions have influenced disclosure practices by preventing the advertising of rates of charge which might be confused with rates representing simple interest. As a result, some financing agencies and sellers advertise rates of charge as "dollars per hundred" rather than as a corresponding percentage rate.

4. The result of the varying disclosure practices is that consumers do not obtain easily comparable information from alternative suppliers of credit. Some suppliers give consumers information about finance charges in dollars; some give multiple per cent per month rates on outstanding balances; some give multiple annual rates on amounts borrowed; some give single rates of charge in the form of "dollars per hundred" on amounts bor-rowed (computational equivalents); and some (relatively few) give both rates of charge and dollar charges. Credit unions often give monthly effective rates of charge computed on outstanding

balances in their contracts and sometimes quote annual effective
rates orally. Virtually all credit sources, of course, give consumers
payment information, i.e., the number of instalment payments
and the size of each payment.

5. A review of the mathematics required to convert dollar charges
   to effective (compound) monthly and annual rates suggests that
   most credit purchasers would be either unable or unwilling to
   make these calculations. Similarly, they would be either unable
   or unwilling to convert computational rate information (i.e.,
   rates used to compute the finance charge, generally applied to
   the original balance) to effective rates, using any but the simplest
   conversion formulas.

6. For consumers to make effective comparisons of alternative
   credit opportunities, ideally they need to know:
   a. The dollar amount of finance charges.
   b. The size and number of monthly payments.
   c. The computational rate(s) used to calculate finance charges.
   d. The effective finance rate together with the compounding
      interval used in its computation.
   Each of these forms of information contributes to certain comparisons of credit alternatives. None, by itself, can serve effect-
   ively as a single criterion because each one applies only to some
   aspect of credit decisions.

7. A review of empirical studies on the extent of borrowers' information about finance charges indicates that:
   a. Consumers have little knowledge of the level of charges or
      rates, when asked about their most recent instalment pur-
      chase or loan. Information about dollar charge is more fre-
      quently found among lower-income groups and information
      about finance rates among higher-income groups.
   b. Consumers consistently underestimate the finance rate actu-
      ally paid, and the extent of understatement tends to be
      greater the higher the rate. However, the fact that both es-
      timated and actual rates vary together implies that rate
      knowledge, although small, is not wholly absent.
   c. More consumers appear to know the computational rate than
      the effective annual rate, the former being much the lower

figure. Only 18 per cent of a subsample of credit users in the Consumers Union-National Bureau 1960 survey gave a reasonably accurate estimate of either the computational rate or the effective annual rate. About 7 per cent were able to approximate the effective annual rate actually paid, while about 11 per cent gave a figure close to the authors' estimate of the computational rate.

   d. Most borrowers do not appear to be sensitive to changes in finance rates, although those with substantial liquid assets, higher incomes, and unfavorable attitude toward debt are more apt to be than those with few liquid assets, lower incomes, and a favorable attitude toward debt.

8. The preceding findings reveal that a great variety of useful information is given consumers, but the variety precludes any easy comparison of many kinds of credit alernatives. The merits and limitations of the relevant types of finance charge information can be summarized as follows:

   a. *Dollar charge and monthly payment* information have definite advantages for comparisons among credit transactions with the same maturity, especially for goods with different prices and different finance charges. They have definite limitations for comparisons among transactions with different maturities and when the use of liquid assets in place of borrowing is possible.

   b. *Computational rates,* normally expressed on a per annum basis, facilitate comparison of credit costs for alternative maturities *provided such rates are all cast in the same form.* Different forms of computational rates are only roughly comparable at best. For comparison with yields on liquid assets, computational rates need to be converted to effective annual rates.

   c. *Effective rates,* whether computed from dollar charges or from a computational rate, are cumbersome to calculate on an actuarial or annuity basis. It is likely that some substitute formula that would be easier to use, such as the direct-ratio or constant-ratio formula, would offer a more convenient means of approximating the actuarially correct rate. Rate tables or charts based on any of these formulas represent a further short cut in determining finance rates. Whether computed with an annuity or approximate formula or a rate chart, an effective rate provides the most accurate comparison of credit transactions that have different maturities or involve a choice between liquidating assets and borrowing. Effective rate comparisons should, however, be used with caution whenever they involve short-maturity instalment contracts for small amounts or when the same commodity, e.g., a new car, may be purchased at different prices.

2 . Methods of Computing and Quoting Finance Charges

FINANCE CHARGES may be computed in one way and quoted in another way or not quoted at all. All credit grantors use a rate of charge to compute dollar charges. Some quote only that rate, some quote both the rate and the dollar amount of the charge, some quote only the dollar amount, and some do not quote charges at all.

This chapter describes the three general methods which financing agencies and sellers use in computing finance charges; traces the evolution of these methods in instalment cash lending and retail instalment financing; indicates the extent to which they and their variants are specified in state legislation; and describes recent trends in computational methods used in revolving credit and small loans; and discusses the ways in which financing agencies and sellers quote finance charges to consumers.

The term finance charge is used throughout this paper to mean the dollar charge or charges for consumer credit excluding (1) any filing and recording fees which financing agencies and sellers collect from credit users for payment to public officials and (2) any charges on insurance written in connection with a credit transaction. In data compiled by the National Bureau and presented in this study, filing and recording fees and insurance premiums are included in the amount of credit extended, when financed, rather than in the finance charge.

Finance charges have various other trade names. In retail instalment financing they are called credit service charges, carrying charges, and time-price differentials, and in instalment cash lending they are called interest charges.

The term finance rate is used to mean the finance charge expressed as an effective annual rate, i.e., as a percentage of the average unpaid balance of the credit contract during its scheduled life. The term monthly finance rate is used to mean the finance charge expressed as an effective monthly rate.

Methods of Computing Finance Charges

THE THREE GENERAL METHODS

The three general methods used by financing agencies and sellers in computing finance charges and by states in setting finance charge ceilings apply rates of charge either to the amount borrowed or to the amount outstanding. These methods are commonly known as add-on, discount, and per cent per month on declining balance.

The add-on and discount methods apply rates of charge to the amounts borrowed. When expressed as percentages, they are called add-on and discount rates. When expressed in dollars and cents per some unit of the amount borrowed, e.g., per $100, they are called computational equivalents because they give the same finance charge as comparable rates. Thus an add-on rate of 7 per cent and an add-on computational equivalent of $7 per $100 borrowed produce the same finance charge. The per cent per month method of computing finance charges applies rates of charge at the end of each month to the credit balance outstanding during the month.

In describing the historical development and present status of the three general computational methods, it is convenient to consider instalment cash lending and retail instalment financing separately.

HISTORICAL DEVELOPMENT: INSTALMENT CASH LENDING

The prevailing social attitude toward instalment cash lending during, and even before, the nineteenth century played a vital role in influencing methods of computing finance charges for cash loans. This attitude was largely negative when consumer demand for loans developed in the decades after the Civil War. It stemmed from our European Christian heritage which once condemned all money lending for interest and then gradually condoned the practice provided the interest did not exceed a socially accepted ceiling set by law. Such a law is called a usury law and applies to all forms of lending not specifically exempted.

Most usury laws contain two ceilings, a legal ceiling and a contract ceiling. The legal ceiling is the maximum annual interest rate which may be charged in any loan contract which fails to specify an interest rate. The contract ceiling is the maximum annual interest rate which may legally be contracted for in any loan transaction. The contract ceiling is usually higher than the legal ceiling and is the one we are concerned with here. Both ceilings, it should be emphasized, are construed by courts to mean effective annual interest rates or yields. An effective annual rate is the finance or interest charge expressed as a percentage per year of the average unpaid balance of the loan or credit.

Forty-seven states and the District of Columbia have had usury laws during all or most of their existence. Table 1 contains 1964

TABLE 1

Frequency Distribution of State Contract Usury Ceilings and
Method of Expressing These Ceilings, 1964

Contract Usury Ceiling (per cent per year)	Number of States[a]	Number of States[b] Expressing Usury Ceiling in	
		Per Cent	Dollars Per $100
6	11	5	6
7	5	2	3
8	13	7	6
9	1	—	1
10	12[b]	12	—
12	5	4	1
30	1	—	1
Total with ceiling	48	30	18
Total with no ceiling	3		

a Including the District of Columbia.
b Including New Mexico, whose ceiling is 10 per cent on secured loans and 12 per cent on unsecured loans.

usury ceilings (as contract ceilings are called from here on) and gives a general picture of those which prevailed earlier, for there have been relatively few changes in usury ceilings over the years.

In the main, the usury ceilings in these laws were too low to enable commercial banks to make consumer loans on a profitable basis. Pawnbrokers and a few remedial loan societies were the only other legitimate lending agencies [1] in existence until around 1910 and they were unable to satisfy the rising demand for loans. Consumer lending was driven underground rather than eliminated because consumer demand was insistent and rising and society was unwilling to legislate sufficiently high ceilings to enable widespread legitimate lending on a profitable basis.

Illegal lenders grew in number and dominated consumer lending during the underground period, known as the loan-shark period, which extended from the Civil War to around World War I. They charged high rates, used a multiple advance charge method of computing finance charges, encouraged short maturities to stimulate refinancing and delinquency charges, gave no prepayment refunds, and adopted strict collection practices.[2]

Illegal lenders adopted a multiple charge system, in part at least to attempt to "comply" with the usury laws. The part they called interest was usually equal to or less than the relevant usury ceilings. In the absence of legislative sanction, courts usually regarded the other parts of the finance charge (service charges and fees) as interest and ruled the transaction usurious whenever the total charge exceeded the relevant usury ceiling.

A number of cities vainly attempted to drive out illegal lenders during the 1880's and the 1890's. Illegal lenders stopped lending during the drives but resumed after they had ended.[3]

The failure of these drives forced growing recognition of the fact that consumer lending was here to stay. The choice was not between lending and no lending but between lawful and unlawful lending. Social attitudes change slowly and are often colored in un-

---

[1] As used here, "legitimate lending agency" means an agency which made loans at finance rates not higher than the legal ceiling under which it operated. For another use of the term, see Louis N. Robinson and Rolf Nugent, *Regulation of the Small Loan Business*, New York, 1935, p. 56.

[2] Multiple advance charges and prepayment refunds are defined in the glossary at the end of this book, and the latter are also discussed below.

[3] See, for example, Arthur Ham, *The Chattel Loan Business*, New York, 1909, Chap. 4; Earle E. Eubank, "The Loan Shark in Chicago," *Bulletin of the Department of Public Welfare, City of Chicago*, November 1916, p. 32; Samuel McCune Lindsay, "Loan on Salaries and Wages," *The American Review of Reviews*, December 1909, pp. 725–726; and J. T. Exnicjos, "The Usury Evil in the City of Washington," *U.S. Senate Document No. 23*, 60th Congress, 2nd Session, Washington, 1911, pp. 5–6.

expected ways by events. The excesses of illegal lenders strengthened a widening conviction that profit-making lenders could operate only at what were then regarded as excessive rates. Before 1900 some twelve states sought to encourage profit-making lenders by passing laws permitting the lending of relatively small sums at ceiling rates in excess of usury ceilings. The ceilings in these laws were too low, however, to permit profit-making lenders to operate on a profitable basis and the laws failed to accomplish their objective. Emphasis gradually shifted from profit-oriented to consumer-oriented agencies as the best means of supplanting illegal lenders.

The terms consumer-oriented and profit-oriented are used in a descriptive rather than a normative sense. A profit-oriented firm has to make a profit in a private enterprise economy, such as ours, in order to survive. While not uninterested in consumers, it cannot consider them to the exclusion of its owners (shareholders) and expect to continue in business. A consumer-oriented firm is under little or no compulsion to make profits and therefore shifts its point of view almost entirely toward serving the consumer. It may do a better or worse job than a profit-oriented firm in serving consumers, for factors other than orientation affect performance.

Remedial Loan Societies and Credit Unions. Remedial loan societies were the first of two types of consumer-oriented agencies. The initial society was organized in 1857, the second in 1888, and thirteen additional ones between 1894 and 1909.[4] The National Federation of Remedial Loan Associations was formed in 1909, two years after the Russell Sage Foundation became active in consumer finance. These two organizations worked closely together to organize new remedial loan societies and to develop principles on which to base consumer finance legislation.

Credit unions were the other type of consumer-oriented agency. The first one was organized in 1909. The number grew slowly until 1921 when Edward Filene established and financed the Credit Union National Extension Bureau to promote the organization of credit unions on a national scale. Before that, most credit unions were located in Massachusetts and New York. The Russell Sage Foundation drafted the New York credit union law, which was

4 Robinson and Nugent, *Regulation of Small Loan Business,* pp. 79–80.

passed in 1913, and actively promoted credit unions in New York after its passage.[5]

Remedial loan societies and credit unions were, for the most part, organized under special laws which usually set ceilings above usury ceilings but below the general level of charges of illegal lenders. The main concern here is with their method of computing finance charges and the reasons for adopting this method, which was used initially by some (not all) remedial societies and credit unions and became more or less standard practice after 1909 under the leadership of the Russell Sage Foundation and the National Federation of Remedial Loan Associations.

The central problem of illegal lending was the level of finance charges, including not only original finance charges but also service, refinancing, and delinquency charges and failure to make prepayment refunds. Remedial societies and credit unions gradually worked out a method of computing charges which, in their opinion, minimized consumer exploitation and misunderstanding. This was per cent per month on declining balance.

According to this method (also called the simple interest method and true interest method), the finance or interest charge is computed at the end of each month by applying a monthly percentage rate to the loan balance outstanding. Thus, if the loan balance during June is $200 and the monthly rate is 2 per cent, the finance charge for June is $4.

The reasoning behind the choice of this method by remedial loan societies and credit unions may be summarized as follows. The finance charge is computed monthly because, since consumers generally make monthly instalment payments, the month was viewed as the natural interval in consumer instalment lending. Computing the finance charge at the end of the month (1) makes special delinquency charges unnecessary since the borrower pays at the regular finance charge rate for each day he uses the money, (2) avoids the need of prepayment refunds on loans which are paid in full before maturity, and (3) simplifies refinancing since loans may be enlarged, extended, or reduced without the need of prepayment refunds. All these characteristics, it should be noted, are

5 *Ibid.*, pp. 90, 152–153.

inherent in a method which computes the finance charge at the end of each instalment period.

As developed by the Russell Sage Foundation and the National Federation of Remedial Loan Associations, per cent per month on declining balance provides one single over-all charge intended to cover all cost elements involved in financing. These elements can be classified in various ways and include capital acquisition cost, service cost, and risk. The one over-all charge was conceived as a means of making it easy for borrowers to ascertain the finance cost as an effective monthly rate and of preventing financing agencies from charging extra fees. The one-charge feature, it should be noted, is not inherent in the per cent per month method. It can be made part of any method of computation.

After the Russell Sage Foundation and the National Federation of Remedial Loan Associations began encouraging the formation of remedial societies in 1909, the number increased to forty-one within several years. Leaders of the National Federation thought the societies would multiply sufficiently to take care of the consumer loan demand.

Whether the Russell Sage Foundation shared this view at any time is not entirely clear. The societies were critical of the Foundation's shift in emphasis from organizing remedial societies to promoting the passage of small-loan laws which would encourage lawful consumer lending by profit-oriented financing agencies. The Foundation made the shift somewhere around 1911 when it realized that remedial societies and credit unions were not multiplying sufficiently to meet more than a small fraction of the consumer loan demand. A Foundation spokesman later stated that the Foundation never expected remedial societies to take over the whole job. "They were intended as experimental agencies—an object lesson—a stabilizing force. . . ." [6]

Of importance here is that the Foundation advocated the inclusion of the method of per cent per month on declining balance in small-loan laws passed before 1916 and incorporated it in the Uniform Small-Loan Law which was drafted in 1916 in cooperation with the newly formed National Association of Small-Loan Brokers

[6] Arthur Ham, *Small Loan Legislation*, New York, 1922, p. 3.

as a model for legislative guidance. It advocated this method as a natural outgrowth of its study of and experience with lending conditions. It was convinced that lending abuses would be minimized if profit-oriented lenders were required to follow the method of computing finance charges developed by remedial societies and credit unions. The Foundation was successful in getting most of the states which adopted small-loan legislation to follow its point of view, except for the few states which had set usury ceilings in their constitutions. The legislatures in these states had to choose between not passing any small-loan law pending a constitutional amendment or passing a small-loan law using add-on plus or discount-plus methods of computing finance charges.

In a literal sense, per cent per month results in uneven monthly payments, for each succeeding monthly payment is the sum of a fixed repayment of principal and a declining interest payment. Lenders can, however, adopt an alternative procedure which results in even monthly payments. To illustrate this procedure, in a twelve-month loan of $120 at 2 per cent per month, the $120 may be thought of as the present value of twelve periodic payments at a compound interest rate of 2 per cent per period. Using an annuity table, we proceed as follows: (1) the monthly payment under a twelve-month contract whose present value at a compound interest of 2 per cent per month is $1 is $0.09456; (2) the monthly payment under a twelve-month contract whose present value at a compound interest of 2 per cent per month is $120 ($120 × .09456) is $11.35. The even monthly payment is $11.35.

Industrial Banks. The discount method (and its variant, the discount-plus method) of computing finance charges also resulted largely from the adverse social attitude toward money lending which prevailed in the nineteenth century. According to the discount method, the finance charge (F) equals the annual discount rate (D) times the principal amount of credit (P) times the number of years in the contract (N), or $F = DPN$. In the case of the computational equivalent, $F = D'P'N$, where D' is the annual discount in dollars per $100 of principal, and P' is P divided by 100.

If the principal amount is $1,000 and the annual discount rate is 7 per cent, the finance charge is $70 on a one-year contract and

$140 on a two-year contract. The same charges are obtained for an equivalent discount charge of $7 per $100.

The finance charge is deducted from the principal. The credit user receives the difference between the principal and the finance charge and pays back the principal in monthly (or other periodic) instalments. In the above example of a two-year contract, the credit user gets $860 and pays back $1,000 in twenty-four monthly payments of $41.67 each.

According to the discount-plus variant, the finance charge equals an amount computed under the discount method plus an additional charge variously called an investigation charge, service charge, or fee. In formula form:

$$F = DPN + S \text{ or } D'P'N + S$$

where S is the investigation charge, service charge, or fee.

The additional charge comes in several basic patterns: (1) as a flat function of the principal owed, e.g., 2 per cent or $2 per $100; (2) as a sliding function of the principal owed, e.g., 8 per cent on the first $600 and 4 per cent on any excess; or (3) as a function of both the principal and time, e.g., 50 cents per month on the first $50 of principal plus 25 cents per month on each of the next five $50 units of principal. Patterns 1 and 2 contain an absolute dollar limit in some cases.

As a rule, the finance charge (discount and additional charge combined) is subtracted from the principal, as described above for the discount method. An alternative, and reportedly little-used, procedure is to add the additional charge to the principal. The credit user gets this sum less the discount at the time the credit is extended and pays back this sum in monthly instalments. To illustrate this alternative, if the additional charge on a one-year $1,000 contract at a 6 per cent annual discount rate is $20, the principal is $1,020, the discount is $61.20 (6% × $1,020), the cash or its equivalent to the credit user is $958.80 ($1,020 − $61.20) and the monthly payments are $85 ($1,020 ÷ 12).

Arthur Morris became aware of the demand for consumer loans during his legal practice. When he set up what is recognized as the first industrial bank [7] in 1910 to help meet this demand, he was

---

[7] The term industrial comes from the fact that consumer loans were originally made mainly to industrial workers. Industrial banks are also called industrial

familiar with the discount method traditionally used by commercial banks in lending to business firms. To obtain an effective rate high enough to make small loans without benefit of a special statute, he combined a discount loan at a legal rate under the usury laws with a repayment plan in a hypothecated savings account. It is thus fairly clear that the use of the discount method in instalment cash lending is the result of its earlier use in business lending and the desire to secure a maximum return under usury restraints.[8]

According to the method worked out by Morris, an industrial bank entered into two simultaneous but legally unrelated contracts with each borrower. One was a loan contract at a discount rate within the usury ceiling whereby the borrower agreed to pay back the principal of the loan at maturity. As the borrower received an amount less than the principal, the difference represented the discount plus a service or investigation charge or fee. The second contract was an investment contract in which the borrower agreed either to purchase an investment certificate or build up a savings account equal to the loan principal by making equal monthly payments over a period equal to the loan period. Neither the investment certificate nor the savings account earned interest before they were used to retire the principal of the loan at maturity.

Society's skeptical attitude toward consumer lending during the formative years of industrial banking undoubtedly helps explain why industrial bank spokesmen so long denied that their plan resulted in finance charges which, from an economic standpoint, exceeded usury ceilings. Lacking legislative sanction, they needed court sanction and were probably fearful of giving courts ammunition which might cause an adverse ruling on the plan's legality. The plan raised two legal points. First, were the two contracts separate or were they, in fact, part of one transaction? Second, was the investigation or service charge separable from interest or was

---

loan companies, industrial loan and investment companies, "Morris Plan" banks, consumer discount companies, industrial savings banks, and industrial loan and thrift companies.

8 A few remedial loan societies adopted the discount method in consumer financing before Morris did. They did so under special legislation authorizing rates in excess of usury rates. They had little influence on the subsequent spread of the discount method, however, for most remedial loan societies used per cent per month and the remedial loan movement advocated per cent per month.

it a disguised added interest charge? Most of the courts which considered these points ruled the plan legal.

As industrial banks became established and multiplied, many states gave them firmer legal standing by passing industrial loan laws authorizing ceiling charges above usury ceilings and exempting industrial banks from the usury laws. Two points are of particular importance here. First, most of these laws set ceilings in terms of discount plus as devised by Morris or, in a few cases, in terms of its close counterpart, discount. Some of the laws that adopted the discount method set a discount rate which was the sum of the previously existing discount and service charge rates. Second, many of the laws adopted a maximum discount rate which was the same as that state's usury ceiling rate.

Maximum revenue was important for, even with discount plus, Morris' plan gave maximum finance rates which were lower than those allowed in remedial, credit union, and small-loan laws. The result was a separation of the market into two parts with an unknown overlap. Industrial banks made larger lower-cost loans, and credit unions, remedial societies, and small-loan companies made smaller higher-cost loans. Some remedial loan society leaders used these facts as the basis for their claim that industrial banks were no solution to the loan-shark problem.[9]

Per cent per month on declining balance and discount plus became firmly established as legal lending increasingly replaced illegal lending in the years after 1910. Remedial loan societies, credit unions, and small-loan companies generally used per cent per month on declining balance and industrial banks generally used discount plus. Commercial banks also tended to adopt discount plus or discount when they entered consumer lending in the 1930's. They did so for a variety of reasons: (1) discounting was the traditional method of computing commercial loan charges; (2) entering without benefit of special legislation, they faced the same situation which Morris had faced twenty years earlier; and (3) the 1934 original FHA Title I repair and modernization loan plan, which influenced many banks to enter consumer lending, promulgated a

9 W. N. Finley, "Report of the Chairman," *Bulletin of the National Federation of Remedial Loan Associations*, August 1913, p. 3.

regulation setting a maximum rate of ". . . $5 discount per $100 original face value of a 1-year note to be paid in equal monthly instalments, calculated from the date of the note. . . ." [10]

States began adding legislative sanction in the 1930's by passing instalment or personal loan laws exempting commercial bank consumer instalment cash lending from the usury laws. Most instalment loan laws specify discount plus or discount; over half have ceiling discount rates which are the same as the relevant usury ceiling rates.

HISTORICAL DEVELOPMENT: RETAIL INSTALMENT FINANCING

Although a credit sale and a loan of money to purchase consumer goods are similar economically, they are quite dissimilar legally. Most courts in the United States have held that credit extended for the sale of a product is not a loan of money and therefore does not come under the jurisdiction of the usury laws.[11]

This doctrine is called the time-price doctrine and is based on the following reasoning. A seller can sell goods for cash or credit. He can, if he wishes, have two prices, a cash price and a credit price. The cash price applies to the sale of goods under one set of specified conditions and the credit price under another set of specified conditions. Both are straight sale transactions and neither come under the usury laws since neither involves an advance of money. The difference between the cash and credit prices is often called the time-price differential.

In developing the time-price doctrine, courts have also developed certain exceptions to it, which cover credit sales made under the following conditions: (1) when the seller fails to quote both a cash and a credit price; (2) when the seller and a financing agency agree

---

10 J. D. Coppock, *Government Agencies of Consumer Instalment Credit,* New York, National Bureau of Economic Research, 1940, p. 51, fn. 29.

11 See William D. Warren, "Regulation of Finance Charges in Retail Instalment Sales," *Yale Law Journal,* April 1959, pp. 840–843. Arkansas and Nebraska courts are the main exceptions here and then mainly in recent years. See *ibid.,* pp. 849–851, and "Nebraska Instalment Sales Act of 1959 Ruled Unconstitutional by Supreme Court," *Personal Finance Law Quarterly Report,* fall 1963, pp. 131–132. Nebraska may be a temporary exception for it adopted a constitutional amendment in 1964 empowering the legislature to enact retail instalment financing legislation.

before a sale that the agency will purchase the buyer's contract from the seller; and (3) when a close relationship exists between the seller and the financing agency.[12] On the first point, the time-price doctrine applies if the seller has both a cash and a credit price, even though he computes the credit price by starting with the cash price and adding an amount to it. Courts universally hold that credit sales which do not come under the doctrine are subject to the usury laws.

The time-price doctrine is a legal concept. Its economic rationale is questionable because most instalment sellers do not have one credit price. They have a number of credit prices, often one for each possible contract maturity. From an economic point of view, these credit transactions can be regarded as the equivalent of the advance of funds for different periods of time rather than as the sale of goods under different conditions of sale. A number of legal observers have questioned the logic of the doctrine.[13]

Retail instalment financing goes back a long way but became significant mainly after World War I when automobiles and household appliances became increasingly important to consumers. Although skeptical views of the social and economic worth of retail instalment financing were widely held well into the 1930's,[14] no legal barriers to the natural development of such financing were erected. The time-price doctrine enabled instalment sellers to establish finance charges without regard to usury ceilings and to develop their own methods of computing such charges.

The finance charge practices of instalment sellers were undoubtedly influenced in many cases by the buying-rate policies of sales finance companies. Buying rates were discount rates applied to the face amount of the paper (including the finance charge of the instalment seller to the instalment buyer) which finance companies

12 Warren, *Yale Law Review*, April 1959, pp. 843–849.

13 See *ibid.*, pp. 848–849, and Raoul Berger, "Usury in Instalment Sales," *Law and Contemporary Problems*, April 1935, pp. 148–172. The Mosaic code, Papal decretals, and court decisions in European countries have generally applied usury restraints both to the loan of money and the loan of goods. For a defense of the time-price doctrine, see Stanley B. Ecker, "Commentary on 'Usury in Instalment Sales,'" *Law and Contemporary Problems*, April 1935, pp. 173–188.

14 See, for example, Roger Babson, *The Folly of Instalment Buying*, New York, 1938, and Edwin R. A. Seligman, *Economics of Instalment Selling*, New York, 1927, Vol. 1, Chap. 12.

purchased from instalment sellers.[15] It is, therefore, worthwhile looking at both finance charge and buying-rate practices in the years following World War I. Studies indicate that sellers who made a separate identifiable charge for instalment credit generally used one or more variations of the add-on method in the years following World War I and, presumably, in the preceding years as well.[16] For convenience, we call these variations flat charge, flat add-on, variable add-on, and annual add-on.

In all of these variations, and two more which are introduced later, the finance charge is added to the principal. The credit user receives the principal and pays back the sum of the principal and the finance charge in monthly or other periodic instalments. To illustrate, if the principal of a one-year instalment contract is $100 and the add-on finance charge is $8, the credit user receives $100 and pays back $108 in twelve monthly instalments of $9.

In the flat add-on charge, a flat dollar charge is made for the credit regardless of the length of the credit period. The following actual examples from the 1920's may be cited: a washing machine manufacturer charged $10 for financing the instalment sale of his washing machines and a sewing machine manufacturer set a cash price of $83.10 and an instalment price of $96 for his sewing machines.[17]

Mail-order companies used variable add-on rates.[18] Sales finance companies used flat, variable, and annual buying rates to determine the charges which they made in buying instalment receivables from sellers.[19] A flat add-on rate is a percentage rate which is the same for contracts of all maturities. Variable rates are percentage rates which vary but not as a proportionate function of time, viz.: [20]

[15] Otto C. Lorenz and H. M. Mott-Smith, *Financial Problems of Instalment Selling,* New York, 1931, p. 94.

[16] For examples in the 1920's, see Wilbur C. Plummer, *Social and Economic Consequences of Buying on the Instalment Plan,* Supplement to the *Annals of the American Academy of Political and Social Science,* January 1927, p. 30.

[17] *Ibid.*

[18] Lewis A. Froman, "The Cost of Instalment Buying," *Harvard Business Review,* January 1933, p. 234.

[19] See Lorenz and Mott-Smith, *Financial Problems,* pp. 93–96; Plummer, *Buying on Instalment* Plan, p. 29; and Seligman, *Instalment Selling,* p. 288.

[20] *Ibid.,* p. 288.

Maturity in Months	Percentage Rate
4	5
6	6½
8	8
10	9½
·12	11

An annual add-on rate is applied to each year's portion of a contract or fraction thereof and yields finance charges which are proportionate to time. If the annual add-on rate is 5 per cent, the finance charge on a $100 instalment credit contract is $5 for one year, $10 for two years, and $2.50 for half a year.

In formula form, the finance charge (F) is computed as follows with annual add-on:

$$F = APN \quad \text{or} \quad F = A'P'N$$

where A is the annual add-on rate, P is the principal amount of credit at the start of the contract, N is the number of years in the credit contract, A' is the annual add-on equivalent in dollars per $100 of principal ($A \times \$100$), and P' is P divided by 100.

Finance companies furnished instalment sellers with buying rates in the form of schedules or charts and also included examples to guide sellers in computing finance charges to consumers.[21] To illustrate, one finance company, which had variable buying rates from 4 per cent on four-month paper to 8 per cent on twelve-month paper, suggested that on a ten-month contract the instalment seller compute the finance charge by adding 10 per cent to the selling price.[22] A 10 per cent add-on rate was higher than any of the finance company's buying (discount) rates and was more than sufficient to cover the finance company's charge. In the early 1930's, financing agencies systematized their guidance by furnishing sellers with finance charge charts or tables containing suggested finance charges in dollars. These charges were usually computed by using add-on rates.

The main reason that finance companies suggested that sellers use add-on in preference to discount rates in computing finance

[21] Plummer, *Buying on Instalment Plan*, p. 27.
[22] *Ibid.* For other examples, see Seligman, *Instalment Selling*, pp. 288–289, and Harold Emerson Wright, *The Financing of Automobile Instalment Sales*, Chicago, 1927, p. 30.

charges to consumers probably lies in simplicity of computation. Simplicity was important because many small sellers were not well versed in financing procedures and practices and obtained help from financing agencies.

In retail instalment financing, the finance charge is easier to compute with add-on than with discount. To illustrate, if a consumer buys an automobile for $2,000 at an annual add-on rate of 7 per cent, the finance charge on a one-year contract is 7 per cent of $2,000, or $140. With an annual discount rate, the seller must advance more than $2,000 to give the buyer take-home credit of $2,000. Determination of this amount and the discount charge requires solving the following formula:

$$H = P - PD$$

where H is the take-home credit, P is the principal owed, and D is the discount rate per year. In our example this works out as follows:

$$\$2,000 = P - .07P$$
$$\$2,000 = .93P$$
$$P = \$2,150.54$$

The finance charge equals $P - H$, in our case, $150.54.

Discounting instalment loans was adopted by industrial and many commercial banks primarily to enable them to get maximum financing revenue under a given usury ceiling. No such compulsion existed in retail instalment financing. If sellers required more financing revenue, all they needed to do was raise the add-on rate.

Data are not available on the extent to which the several variations of add-on were used in the 1920's and early 1930's. The question might be difficult to answer even with data because (1) twelve-month contracts were then frequent if not predominant in auto financing,[23] (2) many flat buying rates were probably set in terms of twelve-month contracts, and (3) where this was true, flat and annual buying rates would lead to similar finance charges.

The annual add-on became increasingly important after the middle 1930's. Among the factors contributing to this trend were the 6 per cent plan of General Motors Acceptance Corporation

---

[23] Wilbur C. Plummer and Ralph A. Young, *Sales Finance Companies and Their Credit Practices*, New York, NBER, 1940, pp. 140–142. Typical maturities in other types of financing varied from six to eighteen months (*ibid.*, p. 147).

and the lengthening of maturities. For sellers, a flat add-on rate becomes increasingly disadvantageous relative to an annual add-on rate as maturities lengthen beyond a year, just as it becomes increasingly advantageous as maturities shorten below a year. The annual add-on method was well established when states began passing retail instalment financing laws and has been incorporated in most of these laws.

Monthly add-on has been incorporated in a few state laws and is similar to annual add-on in that both give dollar finance charges which change proportionately with changes in maturities i.e., with time. With monthly add-on, the finance charge equals the principal times the add-on rate times the number of months in the contract.

PRESENT STATUS

As the previous section indicates, the three general methods of computing finance charges have several variations currently in use which may be catalogued as follows:

1. *Add-On Method*	2. *Discount Method*	3. *Per Cent Per*
a. Annual add-on*	a. Discount*	*Month Method*
b. Monthly add-on*	b. Discount plus*	a. Per cent per month*
c. Annual add-on plus		b. Precomputation
d. Monthly add-on plus		

The starred variations have already been explained. In the annual and monthly add-on plus variations, the finance charge equals an amount computed under the respective add-on variations plus an additional charge variously called an investigation charge, service charge, or fee. Precomputation is explained later in the chapter. For convenience in exposition, all of the eight variations above are hereafter referred to as computational methods.[24]

We have already seen that the per cent per month method is a direct creation of statute and that the discount and add-on computational methods developed as responses of financing agencies and sellers to existing environments. As states began in the 1920's to

[24] The procedure for computing the finance charges for each of the eight variations is explained in the glossary.

enact legislation governing bank instalment lending, they tended to adopt the discount and discount-plus computational methods developed by industrial and commercial banks. Alternatively, as states began enacting retail instalment financing laws from 1935 on, they tended to adopt one of the add-on computational methods developed by sales finance companies and sellers.

Once passed, laws setting ceilings on finance charges influence all financing agencies and sellers who operate under them to adopt the specified computational methods in order to be sure of not violating the ceilings. Financing agencies are under the strongest compulsion to adopt the specified method when laws specify add-on, add-on plus, per cent per month on declining balance, and pre-computation.

Financing agencies and sellers have some latitude in the laws which specify discount and discount plus. They can, if they wish, charge up to the maximum discount rate specified in the law but use the rate as an add-on rather than a discount. They may safely do this because, first, for any given annual rate or dollars per hundred, the discount and add-on methods give the same finance charge in dollars and, second, the size of the credit is larger with add-on than with discount. As a result, the effective monthly or annual rate is lower with add-on than discount no matter what formula is used to compute the effective rate. A creditor clearly charges less than the legal ceiling when he substitutes an add-on for a similar discount rate. No consumer instalment financing law prohibits below-ceiling charges.

State legislation is now widespread. Approximately two-thirds of the states set finance charge ceilings on automobile intsalment sales and approximately one-third have finance charge ceilings on instalment sales of goods other than automobiles. The ceilings apply to all designated retail instalment credit transactions, whether the resulting instalment credit contracts (also called instalment receivables and instalment paper) are kept by instalment sellers or sold by them to instalment sales finance companies, banks, or other financing agencies.

In cash lending, forty-nine states have small-loan laws (governing consumer finance companies), the federal government and forty-four states have credit union laws, four-fifths of the states have instalment or personal loan laws (governing commercial banks and, in some states, other lenders), and almost three-fifths have industrial loan laws (governing industrial banks). All cash lending laws specify the method to be used in computing finance charges.

Since laws have an influence on finance charge computational practices, one measure of the extent of the use of the various computational methods is the number of laws which require each. This and recent shifts in the use of computational methods are covered in the remainder of this section. In so doing, it is worth emphasizing a basic distinction between per cent per month and other computational methods. In the former, the finance charge is computed at the end of each month (or other payment period) on the credit outstanding during that period. In the several add-on and discount methods and precomputation, the finance charge is computed in advance for the whole contract period, i.e., at the time the credit is extended or renewed.

Most Frequently Used Methods. Annual add-on, discount, discount plus, and per cent per month are the computational methods most frequently designated in state laws.

Annual add-on is widespread in retail instalment financing. Over four-fifths of the existing laws with finance charge provisions set ceilings in terms of annual add-on rates or dollar equivalents. Annual add-on is less widespread but still important in instalment cash lending. It is specified in about one-sixth of the instalment loan laws, approximately one-fifth of the small-loan laws, and one industrial loan law. All of the small-loan laws which specify annual add-on have been passed since 1957 and mark what may be a new trend in the small-loan sphere.

Discount and discount plus are important in cash lending and are of negligible importance in retail instalment financing. Discount is specified in almost two-thirds of the instalment loan laws and in several industrial loan and credit union laws. Discount plus is specified in almost two-thirds of the industrial loan laws, about one-tenth of the instalment loan laws, and a few small-loan laws. Discount is specified in one retail instalment financing law and discount plus is none.

Per cent per month on declining balance is important in cash lending and unimportant in retail instalment financing. It is specified in over four-fifths of the small-loan laws, the Federal Credit Union Law, most of the state credit union laws, a few instalment loan laws, a few industrial loan laws, and a few retail instalment financing laws.

Less Frequently Used Methods. These include monthly add-on, monthly add-on plus, annual add-on plus, and precomputation. Monthly add-on is specified in a few retail instalment financing and industrial loan laws and virtually all existing revolving credit laws (explained below). Monthly add-on plus is specified in one industrial loan law and one small-loan law. Annual add-on plus occurs in one retail instalment financing law, a few industrial and small-loan laws, and one instalment loan law. Approximately one-fourth of the small-loan laws which specify per cent per month and all instalment loan laws, industrial loan laws, and retail instalment financing laws which specify per cent per month also authorize precomputation as an alternative method. While monthly add-on and precomputation are relatively unimportant at present, they have been growing in importance in recent years and are discussed further in the next section.

RECENT LEGISLATIVE TRENDS

Monthly Add-On. Increasing numbers of sellers have been extending what is known as revolving credit and over one-fourth of the states have passed revolving credit laws in recent years. An adaptation of the monthly add-on method is used by most sellers in computing finance charges for revolving credit and is specified in virtually all of the revolving credit laws passed to date.

Revolving credit is over-due charge-account credit on which the seller makes a finance charge. Under the usual revolving credit arrangement, the buyer agrees to pay for the use of the credit if he fails to pay for the purchase within the charge-account period normally allowed by the seller. To illustrate, if a customer has a revolving credit account of $400 on the seller's monthly billing date and the seller's monthly add-on rate is $1\frac{1}{2}$ per cent, the finance charge for the next month is $6.00 and the cutsomer agrees to pay a portion of the $406 in the next month. A new charge is made each billing date for the succeeding month. This is an adaptation of the monthly add-on in that the finance charge is computed at the end of each month for that month rather than at the time the credit is extended for the contract period as a whole.

A number of banks have formulated competitive "charge-account" plans for sellers who do not wish to hold their own revolving credit receivables and check-credit plans for borrowers who wish to borrow money by cashing checks up to prearranged amounts. These banks generally use the above adaptation of the monthly add-on to compute finance charges on both types of credit.

Precomputation. Legal authorization of precomputation as an alternative to per cent per month has been most pronounced in small loans mainly since 1951. With precomputation, the finance charge is computed for the instalment contract as a whole and is added to the principal at the time the credit is advanced. The credit user pays back the sum of the principal and the finance charge in monthly (or other periodic) instalments. The finance charge is computed by one of the two per cent per month procedures described above, both of which give the same result.

Annual Add-On. Approximately one-fifth of the small-loan laws permit annual add-on as an alternative to per cent per month or specify annual add-on alone. This trend toward annual add-on dates from 1957 and is even more recent than the trend toward precomputation.

Factors Underlying the Trend Toward Precomputation and Annual Add-On for Small Loans. Consumer finance companies have provided the main impetus behind these trends. As explained below, companies generally (not universally) favor precomputation and annual add-on over per cent per month as means of improving gross revenue, operating efficiency, and borrower relations.[25]

Originally small-loan laws generally specified a flat per cent per month ceiling rate, e.g., 3 per cent. After 1935 a shift took place to graduated (aggregate, combination, or multiple) ceiling rates and all but three small-loan laws now specify two, three, or four ceiling rates.[26] Massachusetts, for example, has a graduated ceiling struc-

25 J. Miller Redfield, "Why Precomputation?" *Personal Finance Law Quarterly Report,* spring 1960, pp. 57–59.
26 For the reasons for this shift, see Wallace Mors, "Rate Regulation in the Field of Consumer Credit," *The Journal of Business,* January 1943, pp. 60–63, and Robinson and Nugent, *Regulation of Small Loan Business,* pp. 267–269.

ture with four rates, viz.: $2\frac{1}{2}$ per cent a month on the part of a loan under $200; 2 per cent a month on the part between $200 and $600; $1\frac{3}{4}$ per cent a month on the part between $600 and $1,000; and $\frac{3}{4}$ per cent a month on the part between $1,000 and $3,000.

Under any given graduated structure, per cent per month, precomputation, and annual add-on can be designed to provide the same gross revenue on loans which are paid on schedule to maturity. Precomputation and annual add-on produce higher gross revenue than per cent per month on prepaid loans, i.e., loans paid in full or refinanced before maturity. The reason for this lies in different procedures for allocating the finance charge to each month of the contract under precomputation and add-on, on the other hand, and per cent per month, on the other.

Virtually all of the relevant small-loan laws require consumer finance companies to use the "rule of 78" (direct-ratio or sum-of-the-digits) allocation procedure when prepayment refunds have to be computed. A prepayment refund schedule is also an earned revenue schedule since what is earned up to a given point in the contract is not refunded and vice versa.[27]

Under the "rule of 78" the finance charge is allocated as follows: First, the numbers of the months in an instalment loan contract are added. In a twelve-month contract, the numbers or digits are 1 through 12 and add to 78 (hence the name "rule of 78") and in a six-month contract the digits are 1 through 6 and add to 21. Second, the finance charge is allocated among successive months by multiplying it by fractions in which the numerators are the numbers of the months in a contract in reverse chronological order and the denominator is the sum of the digits as determined above. On a six-month contract with a finance charge of $42, the revenue allocated to the first month is 6/21 of $42, or $12, and that allocated to the sixth month is 1/21 of $42, or $2. If the loan is pre-

---

[27] The portion of the finance charge which a company actually earns on a prepaid loan is determined by the "rule of 78" procedure, for the refund is determined by that procedure and, as stated above, the refund plus the amount earned equals the finance charge. To prevent any possible misunderstanding, consumer finance companies are free to use any allocation procedure they wish for internal operating purposes. For a description of four such procedures, see John C. Wetzel, "Earned Income Under Precomputation," *Personal Finance Law Quarterly Report,* winter 1957, pp. 7–10.

paid at the end of the first month, the prepayment refund is $30.[28]

The "rule of 78" procedure always results in a falling monthly earned revenue schedule because the finance charge is computed for the contract as a whole at the start and the fractions used to allocate the finance charge fall each month. While the revenue earned each month under per cent per month also falls, it falls more slowly because, under graduated rates, as the loan balance is reduced each month, the parts paid off move successively from the least expensive, to the most expensive, and because the finance charge is computed at the end of each month on the actual loan balance.

Table 2 illustrates this point. If the loan in the table is prepaid at the end of the first month, the per cent per month lender would have earned $6.80 and the precomputation lender $7.60. This is a gross revenue advantage of $0.80 or 11.8 per cent for precomputation. If the loan is prepaid at the end of the second month, the precomputation lender has a gross revenue advantage of $0.66 or 5.5 per cent.

TABLE 2

Allocation of Finance Charge Earned (Gross Revenue) on a Hypothetical
Loan Under Per Cent Per Month and Precomputation [a]

| | | Finance Charge Earned or Gross Revenue (dollars) | | Cumulative Gross Revenue (dollars) | | Added Cumulative Gross Revenue from Precomputation | |
| | | | | | | | Per Cent of Revenue from |
	Month	Per Cent Per Month	Precomputation [b]	Per Cent Per Month	Precomputation	Dollars	Per Cent Per Month
	1	6.80	7.60	6.80	7.60	0.80	11.8
	2	5.20	5.06	12.00	12.66	0.66	5.5
	3	3.20	2.54	15.20	15.20	—	—
Total	6	15.20	15.20				

[a] The hypothetical loan is a three-month loan of $480 at the following graduated rates: 2 per cent on that part of the loan under $200 and 1 per cent on that part of the loan from $200 to $500.

[b] The figures in this column are the result of allocating the finance charge for the contract as a whole to each month according to the "rule of 78" procedure. The sum of the digits is 6 and the successive fractions are $\frac{3}{6}$, $\frac{2}{6}$, and $\frac{1}{6}$.

[28] For a fuller explanation of this procedure, see M. R. Neifeld, "The Rule of 78th—The Sum of the Digits Method for Computing Refunds," *Personal Finance Law Quarterly Report,* winter 1958, pp. 8–10.

The extent of the percentage revenue advantage of precomputation and annual add-on over per cent per month on prepaid loans depends on loan size, maturity, the point in the loan contract at which prepayment occurs, and the percentage difference between the rates in a graduated rate structure. These points can be seen

TABLE 3

Added Gross Revenue from Precomputation as a Percentage of Gross Revenue from Per Cent Per Month for Selected Loan Sizes, Maturities, and Graduated Rates [a]

Payment	Size of Loan (dollars)						
	500	500	500	500	360	500	500
1	12.3	15.8	22.6	33.9	23.1	19.1	24.1
2	3.6	8.6	13.7	31.9	21.1	11.4	22.8
3	—	4.8	10.0	29.9	19.1	6.8	21.5
4		2.3	7.3	27.9	17.0	3.5	20.7
5		0.7	5.5	25.8	15.0	1.1	18.8
6		—	4.1	23.7	13.1	—	17.4
7			2.9	21.6	11.5		16.1
8			1.8	19.5	10.3		14.6
9			1.0	17.4	9.1		13.1
10			0.5	15.2	8.2		11.7
11			0.2	13.0	7.2		10.2
12			—	10.1	6.4		8.8
13				9.3	5.6		7.5
14				7.8	4.9		6.3
15				5.5	4.1		5.3
16				5.3	3.5		4.4
17				4.2	2.8		3.6
18				3.3	2.2		2.8
19				2.5	1.6		2.1
20				1.7	1.0		1.5
21				1.0	0.6		0.9
22				0.6	0.2		0.4
23				0.2	—		0.1
24				—	—		—

[a] Graduated rates used are as follows:

Loan Portion ($)	Monthly Rates (per cent)		
	Cols. 1–5	Col. 6	Col. 7
0–200	2.5	3.0	2.5
200–400	2.0	2.0	2.0
400–500	.5	.5	1.0

Annual add-on gives the same relative results as precomputation for equivalent graduated rates.

in Table 3. First, under any graduated rate structure, the percentage advantage of precomputation over per cent per month increases for any given loan size as maturity lengthens (compare columns 1, 2, 3, and 4), increases for any given maturity as loan size increases (compare columns 4 and 5), and, for any given loan size and maturity, is greatest in the first month and falls steadily each month throughout the contract period.

Second, between two graduated rate structures, the percentage advantage of precomputation over per cent per month becomes greater for any loan size and maturity, the greater is the percentage difference beween the graduated rates in each structure (compare columns 2 and 6 and 4 and 7). The percentage difference between the first two rates in the column 6 rate structure is $33\frac{1}{3}$ (using the highest rate as base) and in the column 2 structure is 20. For any given month, precomputation gives a higher percentage advantage in column 6 than in column 2. Similarly the percentage differences between the last two rates in the column 4 and column 7 structures are, respectively, 75 and 50. For any given month, precomputation gives a higher percentage advantage in column 4 than in column 7.

The absolute level of the rates in a rate structure does not affect the percentage advantage of precomputation over per cent per month. To illustrate, precomputation gives the same percentage advantage over per cent per month on prepaid contracts under both of the following graduated rate structures even though each rate in structure one is one-half the corresponding rate in structure two:

Loan Portion (dollars)	Structure One Monthly Rates (per cent)	Structure Two Monthly Rates (per cent)
0–200	$2\frac{1}{2}$	5
200–400	2	4
400–500	$\frac{1}{2}$	1

A study covering 1950 and 1951 indicates that instalment loans to existing borrowers accounted for 65 per cent of the loans of the consumer finance companies covered.[29] A New York Banking Department study for 1945–57 states that about 80 per cent of all consumer finance company loans in New York are refinanced.[30] Annual reports of the operations of consumer finance companies in Connecticut in 1959 and 1960 show that existing borrowers comprised over 75 per cent of total borrowers. These figures all support the

[29] W. David Robbins, *Consumer Instalment Loans*, Columbus, 1955, p. 82.
[30] *An Analysis of the Licensed Lender Industry, New York State, 1945–1957*, 1958, p. 72.

conclusion that a high proportion of consumer finance company loans are paid in full or refinanced before maturity.[31]

Collection clerks must separate each instalment payment into interest and return of principal and enter each part in the company's records for per cent per month on declining balance. No such separation is necessary for precomputation and annual add-on, which reportedly increases operating efficiency by speeding collections and reducing the possibility of error.[32] Companies claim that borrowers prefer the equal monthly payments they get with precomputation and annual add-on to the uneven ones they may get with per cent per month on declining balance.[33] Borrower preferences have not yet been tested by direct study.

Methods of Quoting Finance Charges

As Table 4 indicates, there is considerable variation in the different sectors of consumer financing in the finance charge disclosure requirements of state laws and in the voluntary disclosure practices of financing agencies and sellers. Methods of finance charge quotation include dollars, computational rates, computational equivalents, finance rates, monthly finance rates, and multiple effective rates. All but the last term have been previously defined. Multiple effective rates may be defined as two or more effective rates on a given credit contract, each rate applying to a given portion or bracket of the contract, not to the contract as a whole.

INSTALMENT CASH LENDING

In cash lending, credit union laws do not require any finance charge disclosure as a rule. Credit unions generally quote monthly finance rates in writing to borrowers and often quote annual rates orally as well.

Most of the small-loan laws derived from the uniform small-loan law of the Russell Sage Foundation require that the instalment

[31] For further discussion of prepayment, refinancing, extension, and delinquency, see Appendix D.

[32] Redfield, *Personal Finance Law Quarterly Report,* spring 1960, p. 58. For an opinion that annual add-on increases efficiency but that precomputation does not, see L. J. Holroyd, Jr., "Precomputation—Is it Really Progress?" *Personal Finance Law Quarterly Report,* winter 1957, p. 15.

[33] Redfield, *Personal Finance,* spring 1960, p. 57.

TABLE 4

Disclosure Requirements of Consumer Financing Laws and Disclosure Practices of Consumer Financing Agencies and Sellers [a]

Consumer Financing and Usury Laws	Credit Sources	Dollar Charge	Computational Add-On or Discount Rate(s)	Computational Add-On or Discount Equivalent(s)	Finance Rates		Multiple Effective Monthly Rates
					Monthly	Annual	
Instalment cash lending							
Credit union laws	Credit unions				V	V	
Industrial loan laws	Industrial banks	V		V			
Instalment loan laws	Commercial banks[b]	V		V			
Small-loan laws	Consumer finance companies						
Flat per cent per month					L		
Graduated per cent per month	Consumer finance companies						L
Annual add-on rate or equivalent	Consumer finance companies		L	L			
Retail instal. financing laws	Instalment sellers	L					
	Sales finance cos.	L					
	Commercial banks	L					
	Other	L					
Revolving credit laws	Instalment sellers				L		L
Usury laws	All lenders						

[a] L = Legal requirements. V = Voluntary practice.

[b] On "check-credit" and "charge account" plans, banks often quote charges on a per cent per month basis.

cash loan contract contain a reproduction of the rate section of the law or the rate or rates being charged for the loan in question. A number of other laws require a similar disclosure. The rate section of a small-loan law specifies computational rates. Publication of rates under the section results in the three following types of finance charge quotation: a monthly finance rate in the few laws which specify a flat per cent per month rate; multiple effective monthly (or yearly) rates in the small-loan laws which have two or more graduated per cent per month (or per year) rates; and computational annual add-on rates or equivalents in the small-loan laws which have two or more graduated add-on rates or equivalents. Four small-loan laws require disclosure of the finance charge in dollars or as a finance rate.

A few instalment loan laws and a few industrial loan laws require that the instalment cash loan contract contain a reproduction of the rate section of the law. At least one instalment loan law and one industrial loan law require that the contract state the computational rate or rates used to compute the finance charge. Most of the laws do not impose any disclosure requirements on industrial and commercial banks. Both types of banks generally follow the practice of quoting charges as a discount (or, in some cases, an add-on) equivalent, i.e., in "dollars per hundred of the amount borrowed."

Dollar disclosure, i.e., expressing the finance charge for an instalment contract as a whole in dollars, is recommended by the American Bankers Association and practiced by many banks. For special bank plans, such as "check credit" and "charge account banking," banks often quote charges as a monthly rate and show the finance charge as a dollar amount on the monthly bill.

RETAIL INSTALMENT FINANCING

Dollar disclosure has been a major feature of retail instalment financing laws since the first law was enacted in 1935 and was recommended as a trade practice rule in auto financing by the Federal Trade Commission in 1951. These laws generally require separate quotation of the finance charge in dollars in a written instalment contract. Other items which must be shown separately in the contract include price, down payment, insurance premiums, other charges, balance owed, number of payments, and amount of each payment. A few laws permit a seller to combine the finance and insurance charges in the contract provided he shows them separately in a (later) written statement to the buyer.

We have already seen that all but one of the retail instalment financing laws with ceilings set ceilings in terms of add-on rates (or equivalents) applied to the amount borrowed. Dealers and financing agencies often disclose add-on equivalents in response to consumer questions about credit costs.[34] Instalment financing laws do not require disclosure of finance rates.

Some revolving credit laws require that the revolving credit agreement contain a reproduction of the rate section of the law. This results in the quotation of a monthly finance rate in the laws which specify a flat per cent per month rate and of multiple effective monthly rates in those laws which have graduated per cent per month rates. Usury laws do not have any disclosure requirements.[35]

LEGISLATIVE PROPOSALS FOR UNIFORMITY IN
METHOD OF FINANCE CHARGE QUOTATION

There have been numerous discussions going back as far as the turn of the century on the subject of providing consumers with uniform finance charge information. Some discussions have been limited to certain sectors of consumer credit while others have included virtually the whole field. Most of them have been in terms of either effective annual or effective monthly rates. We cite only enough of them here to document the point that uniformity in method of finance charge quotation has been and is a subject of continuing interest.[36] Except where otherwise noted, proposals for a uniform method of quotation do not imply or require a uniform method of finance charge computation.

Between 1906 and 1942 the Russell Sage Foundation advocated a

34 As discussed in Chapter 3, court rulings prohibit sellers and nonbank financing agencies from quoting add-on or discount rates. The American Bankers Association has adopted a policy which asks banks to refrain from quoting add-on and discount rates. Most, if not all banks, voluntarily follow this policy.

35 Illinois is an exception here.

36 For additional citations covering 1935–43, see *Opinions of Charges to Consumers for Small Instalment Loans,* Chicago, 1943.

per cent per month method of finance charge computation and quotation for small loans and credit unions. It advocated extension of this method of finance charge computation and quotation to retail instalment financing in 1940 and to personal instalment lending by banks in 1942.[37]

A 1930 study of consumer credit advocates legislation which would require all instalment financing agencies ". . . to calculate their rates on the basis of a single standard of measurement, which would show the percentage per year rate charged the borrower for the funds of which he has the actual use, and to include a statement of this rate in all their loan contracts." [38]

The Consumers' Advisory Board set up under the National Recovery Act of 1933 recommended that provisions be inserted in Retail Trade Codes requiring that monthly instalment credit charges be expressed as a percentage on the current unpaid monthly balance.[39] Legislative committees in a number of states made similar recommendations in the 1930's.[40]

A number of pamphlets issued in the 1930's and 1940's by the Pollak Foundation discuss various aspects of consumer instalment financing and, among other things, suggest the adoption of a uniform method of finance charge quotation for all types of such financing.[41] A 1943 article by Rolf Nugent advocates that banks express their finance charges as an actual simple interest rate.[42] Cox' 1948 study on instalment buying cites a number of writers

[37] See "Russell Sage Foundation Uniform Law to Regulate Instalment Selling" (mimeographed), 1940, and "Russell Sage Foundation Model Law to Authorize and Regulate Personal Loans Made by Banks" (mimeographed), 1942.

[38] Evans Clark, *Financing the Consumer*, New York, 1930, p. 243.

[39] For a full statement of the Board's position in its own words, see William Trufant Foster and LeBaron R. Foster, "Rate Aspects of Instalment Legislation," *Law and Contemporary Problems*, April 1935, pp. 193–194. The Fosters agree with the Board's position.

[40] See, for example, "Indiana Consumer Finance Agencies" (mimeographed), Indiana Department of Financial Institutions, 1936, p. 4; *Report of State Banking Commission and Interim Advisory Legislation Committee to Investigate Finance Companies*, Wisconsin, 1936, p. 42; "Report of Committee on Consumer Credit" (mimeographed), Massachusetts, 1936, chap. 3; and *Retail Instalment Selling*, Maryland Legislative Council, Research Report No. 6, 1940, p. 34.

[41] See, for example, William Trufant Foster and LeBaron R. Foster, *Rate Aspects of Instalment Legislation*, Newton, Mass., 1935.

[42] Rolf Nugent, "Why Not Candor in Small Bank Loans?" *Survey Graphic*, March 1943, p. 7.

who object to the existence of diverse ways of quoting finance charges and expresses his own arguments against effective rate quotation as a possible solution.[43]

Moving to more recent years, a Minnesota committee in 1958 recommended enactment of a law requiring ". . . that in all forms of agreements for consumer credit the amount charged either as interest or as finance charge must be stated in terms of simple interest on an annual basis." [44] The Consumer Credit Labeling Bill introduced into Congress in 1960 and the Truth in Lending Bill introduced into Congress in 1961 and subsequent years both contain a provision requiring quotation of the charge for consumer credit as an effective annual rate. Similar bills have been introduced in a number of states including California, Massachusetts, New Mexico, New Jersey, and Oregon. None of these bills has been enacted. A 1962 study considers the problems involved in the full disclosure of consumer credit cost.[45]

On June 22, 1964, the National Conference of Commissioners on Uniform State Laws announced that it had started a "Project on Retail Installment Sales, Consumer Credit, Small Loans and Usury." This project contemplates studies to draft comprehensive, uniform or model state legislation "on substantially all aspects of consumer credit trade practices, including disclosure of cost of credit, rate controls or ceilings, the time price doctrine and usury, contract provisions, licensing and other means of securing compliance, default procedures including garnishments and their relationship to consumer bankruptcies, and the related fields of credit life and credit disability insurance." [46]

[43] Reavis Cox, *The Economics of Instalment Buying*, New York, 1948, pp. 193–208.

[44] "Report by the Governor's Study Committee on Consumer Credit" (mimeographed), Minnesota, 1958, p. 24.

[45] Sarah C. Wang, *Problems in Implementing Full Disclosure of Consumer Credit Cost*, Economic Research Center, University of Hawaii, 1962.

[46] Release dated August 22, 1964.

3. Consumer Uses of
Finance Charge Information

..

THE DEMAND FOR CONSUMER CREDIT depends on current prices of goods and credit, on credit terms, on consumer incomes and wealth, on expected changes in these factors, and on the time preferences of consumers—i.e., their preferences for present versus future consumption. We are concerned here mainly with the credit price factor.

Consumer response to changes in finance charges is measured by the related changes in the amount of credit demanded, i.e., the price elasticity of the demand for credit. The extent to which consumers take credit cost into account in deciding how much, if any, credit to use and where to get credit depends, in part, on the form in which finance charge information is available to them. As seen in Chapter 2, consumers currently receive such information in different forms in different sectors of consumer financing. This chapter deals with the usefulness of these various forms as measures of credit cost.

Measures of Credit Cost

FINANCE CHARGES IN DOLLARS

Dollar finance charges are relatively easy to adjust for differences in the quoted prices on goods to be financed or dollar amounts to be borrowed since all these quantities are expressed in dollars. Their usefulness as a measure of cost is limited, however, to comparisons of alternative financing opportunities that have a common maturity. Consumers who must accept the maximum maturity available to them in order to secure a monthly payment low enough for them to purchase a desired commodity can compare dollar charges and select their lowest cost alternative.[1]

Dollar finance charges do not provide complete information to credit users who want to compare the cost of credit for shorter contract maturities with that for longer contract maturities. A potential credit user, for example, will know that it costs him x dollars more to finance a credit contract of thirty-six months' maturity than one of thirty months' maturity. He must compute an effective monthly or annual rate on both maturities to discover whether the added dollars represent a higher, lower, or equal rate of charge.

Dollar charges are also difficult for borrowers to use as a standard of credit cost when they wish to compare the cost of borrowing with the return on funds invested in savings accounts, government bonds, or other interest-yielding liquid assets. For this purpose the borrower must compute finance charges as an effective annual rate, the medium usually used in expressing the return or yield on liquid assets.

SIZE AND NUMBER OF MONTHLY PAYMENTS

Comparison of the size of monthly payments on alternative credit opportunities is a useful yardstick for credit cost when the number of payments is the same for a given amount of credit. This limitation is the same as for dollar charges. Within this limitation, monthly payments are superior to dollar charges in one respect, however. When an alternative credit opportunity for the same maturity offers a lower price for the goods purchased but a higher dollar finance charge, the monthly payment comparison directly reveals the more costly alternative.

Monthly payment information is not a useful yardstick for credit cost when alternative credit opportunities involve different maturities and different amounts of credit. Comparison of credit costs in such cases requires that monthly payments be converted first to finance charges in dollars and then to effective monthly or annual rates. Similarly, monthly payment data are not useful for comparing

---

1 The same conclusion holds for consumers who can accept below-maximum-maturity contracts provided they limit their dollar finance charge comparisons to contracts having *the same maturity*.

credit cost with yields on liquid assets. Here again, dollar charges must be converted to effective annual rates, the form in which liquid asset yields are usually quoted.

COMPUTATIONAL RATES OF CHARGE AND COMPUTATIONAL EQUIVALENTS

Add-on, discount, and per cent per month computational rates (or equivalents) are not useful as a measure of comparative credit cost when they are all used at the same time by different financing agencies and sellers. Thus, a 6 per cent annual add-on rate is not the same as a 6 per cent annual discount rate, and neither is the same as a monthly rate of $\frac{1}{2}$ per cent on the unpaid balance. Any one of these three computational rates (or equivalents) could be a useful measure of comparative credit cost if all financing agencies and sellers published rates (or equivalents) based on the same computational method.

Publication of computational rates is not legally acceptable, however, unless they are also effective rates, for courts generally hold that any published finance or interest rate should mean an effective rate. This rules out add-on and discount computational rates, for neither is an effective rate.

Court decisions against the form of rate quotation used in the General Motors Acceptance Corporation's 6 per cent add-on plan are an illustration.[2] When the General Motors Acceptance Corporation advertised this plan in 1935, it clearly labeled the 6 per cent add-on rate as follows: "6% a multiplier—not an interest rate." On the basis of the findings quoted below, the Federal Trade Commission called the plan an unfair trade practice and enjoined it: [3]

The Commission's findings were that the term "6%," when used in connection with monthly payments, was understood by the public to mean 6 per cent simple interest per annum computed on the declining balance as reduced by the monthly payments; but that, as actually carried out, the purchaser paid 6 per cent, 9 per cent, or 12 per cent, as the case might be, on the total amount originally owed, until the final payment was made, resulting in a charge of approximately 11½ per cent simple interest per annum on an original balance as reduced by monthly payments.

[2] See U.S. Circuit Court of Appeals, Second Circuit, August 12, 1940 (114 F. 2d 33), and U.S. Circuit Court of Appeals, June 5, 1941 (120 F. 2d 175).
[3] *Annual Report of the Federal Trade Commission for the Fiscal Year Ended June 30, 1940*, p. 81. The FTC ruling does not apply to banks.

As the quotation indicates, the FTC feared that the 6 per cent rate would be interpreted as an effective rate which, clearly, it was not. Consumers who made this interpretation would be led to underestimate the actual rate of charge.

This possibility of underestimation does not change the fact, however, that the plan increased the competitive atmosphere among sellers and financing agencies in 1936. It did so by teaching the borrowing public a simple method of comparing General Motors Acceptance Corporation's low-cost borrowing plan with other finance plans. Through advertisements the public was instructed to determine the finance charge by adding the unpaid balance and insurance cost and multiplying the sum by 6 per cent for twelve months or by 6 per cent plus or minus $\frac{1}{2}$ per cent for periods more or less than twelve months.[4]

Computational equivalents, i.e., rates of charge in dollars per $100 of the amount borrowed, are close counterparts of computational rates and are used mainly as alternatives to add-on and discount percentage rates. The distinction is nonetheless worth making for there have been no court rulings on the matter of publishing computational equivalents.

The legal distinction between add-on (discount) rates and add-on (discount) equivalents may be a fine one, but distinctions of varying degrees of fineness exist in all lines of activity. The final determination of the legality of the distinction rests with legislatures, government commissions, and the courts.[5]

The use of any single type of computational equivalent (or rate) in quoting credit cost enables consumers to appraise competing opportunities on the basis of comparative rates of charge. They still have to value the goods part of their purchases separately from the credit part and, when the advantages appear to affect one another, must make an adjustment to permit a comparison of the combined goods and credit cost. In order to compare costs with liquid-asset yields, computational equivalents (or rates) must either

[4] For reproduction of the relevant part of an advertisment, see Robert P. Shay, "The Price of New-Automobile Financing," *Journal of Finance*, May 1964, p. 214.

[5] For a discussion of the merits of different computational methods, see Roland Stucki, *Analysis of Instalment Financing Legislation and Practices in Utah*, Salt Lake City, 1956, pp. 26–27.

be converted to effective rates or liquid-asset yields must be converted to computational rates.

Computational equivalents (or rates) have an advantage over dollar charge and monthly payment information in that they are a useful means of comparing credit costs over different time periods. The add-on and per cent per month methods of computing charges are more useful than the discount method in this respect, for the variation in the effective rate equivalents of a given add-on or per cent per month equivalent (or rate) is small within customary maturity periods. Any given discount equivalent (or rate) involves progressively higher effective rates as maturities lengthen and, therefore, is less satisfactory as measure of cost of contracts on varying maturities.[6]

FINANCE RATES

Annual and monthly finance rates provide a common denominator for determining the cost of all credit transactions, regardless of size, maturity, or other characteristics. Annual finance rates may be compared directly with liquid-asset yields. Since monthly finance rates are approximately one-twelfth of equivalent annual finance rates, they must be multiplied by twelve for an approximate comparison with liquid-asset yields.[7]

Annual finance rates on small, short-maturity credit contracts are generally very high even when dollar finance charges are nominal. They are high because such contracts magnify the importance of cost elements (particularly acquisition costs) which are independent of the amount of credit or its maturity. The combination of small dollar finance charges and extremely high effective annual rates make it important that dollar charge information supplement effective annual rate information which, by itself, may be misleading to prospective borrowers. Conversely, on large loans with long maturities (e.g., mortgages) dollar charge quotation reveals that relatively low effective rates of charge represent substantial dollar finance charges, approaching or even exceeding the amount borrowed.

Evidence presented below and in Chapter 5 indicates that annual

6 See Appendix B.
7 See Appendix A.

finance rates on short- and intermediate-term credit are above the rates which most consumers believe to be commonly available. The converse is likely on long-term credit. As noted earlier in the discussion of dollar finance charges, finance rates, whether monthly or annual, will not provide as useful a measure of credit cost as the comparison of monthly payments on contracts of identical size and maturity whenever the selling price of the good is changed by the seller to offset a higher or lower finance charge.

MULTIPLE EFFECTIVE RATES

It is important to distinguish clearly between finance rates and multiple effective rates. A finance rate is an effective monthly or annual rate on a credit contract as a whole. Multiple effective rates are separate (usually two to four) effective monthly or annual rates on different portions of a given credit balance. As an example, a given $800 credit contract may have three brackets and three multiple effective monthly rates as follows: 3 per cent on the bracket under $200; 2 per cent on the bracket from $200 to $600; and 1 per cent on the bracket from $600 to $800.[8]

Multiple effective rates have a much more limited usefulness than finance rates as a measure of credit cost because they do not give the cost of the contract as a whole, but rather separate costs of separate brackets of the contract. They provide a useful measure only if all financing agencies and sellers shift from one effective rate to another at identical credit-size intervals and show similar patterns of variation of effective rates within each credit bracket. They must be converted to an effective annual rate for comparison of the credit cost of a contract as a whole with liquid-asset yields. However, since each multiple effective rate shows the marginal rate on an additional amount borrowed, it can be used directly for comparison with liquid-asset yields when liquid assets might be used to reduce the amount of existing debt or to alter the amount borrowed initially.

8 As indicated in Chapter 2, a number of small-loan laws and a few instalment and industrial loan laws require that financing agencies quote multiple effective rates in credit contracts.

Influence of Finance Charge Information on Consumer Behavior

FINANCE RATE VS. SIZE OF MONTHLY PAYMENT

Considerable attention has been given in the literature to the effect of changes in finance charges, down payments, maturities, and size of monthly payments on the amount of credit demanded. In his 1952 study Avram Kisselgoff discusses the hypothesis that even significant variations in finance charges are not likely to result in a significant change in the amount of commodities purchased on credit.[9] In the absence of empirical data, he suggests that this may be attributable partly to consumer lack of knowledge of the cost of credit but is "mainly due to the fact that the cyclical changes that are likely to occur in finance charges are relatively small and can have very little effect on the amount of the monthly payments." [10]

Empirical evidence has not yet firmly established the degree of cyclical variability of finance charges.[11] Thus, the hypothesis that the demand for credit is little affected by changes in finance charges came to rest heavily upon the mechanical relationship between finance charge changes and the size of the monthly payment. A given percentage change in finance charges causes a much lower (usually negligible) percentage change in monthly payments. Thus, raising the add-on rate from 10 to 12 per cent, or by a fifth, on a twelve-month $300 instalment contract increases the monthly pay-

9 Avram Kisselgoff, *Factors Affecting the Demand for Consumer Instalment Credit*, NBER Technical Paper 7, New York, 1952, p. 18. Along parallel lines, Gottfried Haberler comments as follows in his 1942 study, ". . . the view is now rather generally accepted by economists that the amount people save is not much influenced by changes of a few per cent in the rate of interest which can be earned on savings." (See his *Consumer Instalment Credit and Economic Fluctuations*, New York, NBER, 1942, p. 35.) For an alternative view, see Martin J. Bailey, "Saving and the Rate of Interest," *Journal of Political Economy*, August 1957, pp. 279–305.

10 *Ibid.*, p. 18.

11 Robert P. Shay found that new-auto finance rates moved with open-market borrowing rates between 1953 and 1959. The rise and fall (in basis points) of the new-auto series was somewhat less than short-term open-market rates and somewhat greater than long-term rates. New-auto rates lagged behind the three cyclical turning points consistently. (See Shay's *New-Automobile Finance Rates, 1924–62*, NBER Occasional Paper 86, New York, 1963.)

ment from $27.50 to $28.00, or less than 2 per cent. Doubling the add-on rate from 10 to 20 per cent on the same contract increases the monthly payment less than 10 per cent.

Regulation W, the Federal wartime control of the volume of consumer credit, is evidence of belief in consumer insensitivity to finance charges. It controlled volume by regulating credit terms (down payments and maturities) rather than finance charges. This choice reflects the fact that, in the short run, demand for consumer credit was thought to be relatively inelastic with respect to finance charges and sensitive to credit terms. Higher down payments were expected to deter purchases by consumers who were unable or unwilling to sacrifice liquidity, and shorter maturities would also be a deterrent because of the resulting increase in size of the monthly payment. Thus, reducing maturity by 20 per cent increases monthly payment size by 25 per cent and cutting maturity in half doubles monthly payment size.

A 1964 National Bureau study, based on data collected from a Consumers Union Members' Panel, attempts to measure the relative sensitivities of consumer demand for credit to changes in finance rates and maturities.[12] The sample was divided into sixteen randomly selected variant groups. Each of thirteen groups was sent a hypothetical question that specified four alternative ways in which a stated purchase might be financed. One group was given three alternatives and two groups were given five alternatives. The purchase was identical for all groups, an automobile costing $1,500, after trade-in allowance.

Alternative finance plans consisted of offsetting variations in two of the following: down payments, monthly payments, maturities, and finance rates. For fourteen groups there were alternative variations among down payments, monthly payments, or maturities with the finance rate held constant. (The finance rate was often different between groups, however, i.e., 4, 8, or 16 per cent.) Within each of two groups there were offered alternative variations in finance rates. Respondents were asked to rank the alternatives in order of preference and to indicate which alternatives were unacceptable.

[12] For the details of this analysis, see F. Thomas Juster and Robert P. Shay, *Consumer Sensitivity to Finance Rates: An Empirical and Analytical Investigation*, NBER Occasional Paper 88, New York, 1964.

The study uses two approaches to test elasticities of demand with respect to changes in finance rates and maturities. The traditional approach assumes that consumer demand for credit is primarily a function of required monthly payments. "Since monthly payment size is regarded as the price of the asset, longer maturities with lowered monthly payments amount to lower prices. A change in finance rates influences demand only insofar as it changes monthly payments, holding loan size, downpayment, and maturity constant. Let us label this the monthly payments model." [13] If this approach is correct, a change in finance rates can only change the demand for credit through its effect upon monthly payment size.

The second approach, called the marginal borrowing cost model, assumes that consumer demand for credit is a function of a consumer's marginal rate of return from his investment in assets and his marginal borrowing cost (borrowing rate). For empirical analysis consumers are classified as "rationed" or "unrationed." The latter are those whose marginal borrowing cost is equal to or less than going finance rates of primary (lower-rate) credit sources (i.e., banks and sales finance companies). They can borrow additional amounts at rates about equal to the rates they are paying primary lenders. Rationed consumers are those whose marginal borrowing cost exceeds the going rates of primary lenders. They can borrow additional amounts only from secondary (higher-rate) credit sources. "Defined in another way, rationed consumers are those whose average outstanding debt to primary lenders is less than the amount they would prefer, given the rates charged, and unrationed consumers are those whose actual and preferred debt levels are the same." [14]

Both models have empirically observable implications some of which are in direct contradiction. The marginal borrowing cost model predicts that (1) a finance rate rise confined to primary lenders will reduce the borrowing of unrationed consumers and have no effect on that of rationed consumers and (2) a simultaneous increase in finance rates and maturities will reduce the borrowing of unrationed consumers and increase that of rationed consumers.

13 *Ibid.*, p. 17.
14 *Ibid.*, p. 14.

Under this model, consumer response to changes in finance rates depends on the relative importance of rationed and unrationed consumers.

The monthly payments model predicts that all consumers will increase (decrease) borrowing if maturities lengthen (shorten) irrespective of rate changes. It also predicts that ". . . the elasticity of demand for credit with respect to changes in finance rate can be measured indirectly by the elasticity with respect to changes in minimum monthly payments. If consumers respond only to changes in monthly payments, and if a 100 per cent increase in rates increases monthly payments by 10 per cent . . . , the elasticity of demand for credit with respect to rates must be one-tenth the elasticity with respect to payments." [15] Under this model, the separate elasticities of demand for credit with respect to finance rates and contract maturities are a function of the proportionate effect of the changes in each on monthly payment size.[16]

Table 5 summarizes elasticities of demand from the responses of relevant variant groups in the Consumers Union sample. It shows that the elasticity of demand predicted by the payments model, when the finance rate is held constant, varies from – 0.058 (variant pairs 10–11), to – 0.299 (variant pairs 11–14), to – 0.172 (variant pairs 10–14). The elasticity based on the largest payment difference is – 0.172 and is taken as the most reliable estimate.

The payments elasticity thus estimated, – 0.172, is applied to the difference in minimum monthly payments between other pairs of variants, differences that are a consequence, other things being equal, of differences in the implicit finance rates. . . .

This estimate answers the question, how much variation takes place in what people say they would do as maturities are extended, other things equal. The four independent comparisons of a similarly hypothetical finance rate elasticity shown in Table [5] indicate that the response to rate differences is greater than predicted by the payments model in three of the four cases, variant pairs 6–8, 14–15, and 13–16. The computed finance rate elasticity in the fourth case, variant pair 9–12, though negative, is slightly less than would have been predicted on the basis of the difference in minimum monthly payments. Averaging the four comparisons: the mean

15 *Ibid.*, p. 18.
16 *Ibid.*, p. 19.

predicted elasticity is − .020; the mean observed elasticity is − .047—more than double although still quite small in absolute terms.[17]

TABLE 5

Fraction Accepting One or More Alternative Finance Plans for
Specified Variant Groups, Credit Users Only

Variant Groups		No. of Usable Responses	A	Variant Pairs	Elasticities	
No.	Characteristics				Computed	Predicted by Payments Model
INTEREST (FINANCE) RATE CONSTANT (8%)						
10	Maximum M = 24	261	76.6	10–11	−.058	neg.
11	Maximum M = 36	252	78.2	11–14	−.299	neg.
14	Maximum M = 48	254	84.3	10–14	−.172	neg.
DOWN PAYMENT CONSTANT (0)						
14	(i = 8%)	254	84.3	14–15	−.098	−.034
15	(i = 16%)	252	79.0			
8	(i = 4%)	211	80.6	8–6	−.048	−.029
6	(i = 16%)	255	76.1			
CONTRACT LENGTH CONSTANT						
9	(i = 4%)	265	81.5	9–12	−.005	−.016
12	(i = 16%)	248	81.0			
MONTHLY PAYMENTS CONSTANT ($65.10)						
13	(i = 4%)	246	84.7	13–16	−.036	.000
16	(i = 16%)	263	80.2			

SOURCE: Juster and Shay, *Consumer Sensitivity*, p. 29.
NOTE: A = proportion of respondents accepting one or more of the financing alternatives; M = contracts in months; i = interest (finance) rate.

Juster and Shay believe that the evidence in Table 5 suggests that the monthly payments model, i.e., the traditional approach, may underestimate consumer responses to variations in finance rates. To test this hypothesis further, they divided the sample households into rationed and unrationed groups on three bases: family income and marital status, liquid-asset holdings, and attitude to-

[17] *Ibid.*, pp. 28–32. The figure − .020 is the average of the last four numbers in the last column of Table 5 and the figure − .047 is the average of the last four numbers in the next to last column.

TABLE 6

Estimated Finance Rate and Monthly Payment Elasticity of Demand for
Households Classified as Rationed or Unrationed on Three Bases

	Observed Elasticities		
Variant Numbers	Rationed Households	Unrationed Households	Elasticities Predicted by Payments Model
A. FAMILY INCOME AND MARITAL STATUS[a]			
Monthly Payment Elasticities			
10–11	−.152	+.150	neg.
11–14	−.334	−.420	neg.
10–14	−.231	−.083	neg.
Finance Rate Elasticities			
8–6	−.029	−.099	−.029
9–12	−.048	+.116	−.016
14–15	−.120	−.235	−.034
13–16	−.044	−.068	.000
Average of four	−.060	−.072	−.020
B. LIQUID-ASSET HOLDINGS[b]			
Monthly Payment Elasticities			
10–11	+.054	−.114	neg.
11–14	−.155	−.376	neg.
10–14	−.032	−.226	neg.
Finance Rate Elasticities			
8–6	+.027	−.051	−.029
9–12	−.091	−.029	−.016
14–15	−.014	−.253	−.034
13–16	+.030	−.080	.000
Average of four	−.012	−.103	−.020
C. ATTITUDE TOWARD THE USE OF CREDIT[c]			
Monthly Payment Elasticities			
10–11	−.020	+.009	neg.
11–14	−.426	−.368	neg.
10–14	−.191	−.148	neg.
Finance Rate Elasticities			
8–6	−.024	−.128	−.029
9–12	+.029	−.138	−.016
14–15	−.137	−.276	−.034
13–16	−.014	−.152	.000
Average of four	−.036	−.174	−.020

SOURCE: Juster and Shay, *Consumer Sensitivity*, pp. 35, 38, and 41.

NOTES TO TABLE 6

a

	Income After Tax (dollars)		
Marital Status	Under 8,000	8,000– 10,000	Over 10,000
Married 15 years or less	R	R	U
Married more than 15 years or unmarried	R	U	U

(R = rationed, U = unrationed)

b Rationed consumers are those with less than $2,000 in checking accounts, savings accounts, and savings bonds; unrationed are those with $2,000 or more.

c Rationed consumers were those who indicated they intended to use consumer credit in the future and unrationed ones were those who indicated they did not intend to use consumer credit in the future.

ward the use of consumer credit. Table 6 gives the observed elasticities for the rationed and unrationed groups on each of the three bases and also the elasticities predicted by the payments model. On all three bases the results are generally more consistent with the marginal borrowing cost model than with the payments model as follows: (1) except for the liquid-asset classification, rationed consumers respond more to differences in minimum monthly payments than do unrationed ones; (2) unrationed consumers are more sensitive to finance rates; (3) for the most part a combination of higher rates and longer maturities, minimum monthly payments declining on balance, increases the borrowing of rationed consumers and decreases the borrowing of unrationed consumers.[18]

Juster and Shay conclude that their results ". . . clearly indicate the necessity for qualification of the widely held view that consumer borrowing decisions are unresponsive to changes in finance rates, aside from the effect of rate changes on monthly payments. This generalization appears to be valid for rationed consumers . . . [but] is not valid for unrationed consumers." [19]

18 *Ibid.*, pp. 33–40. The authors attach little importance to the perverse behavior of the monthly payments elasticities in the liquid-asset classification in Table 6. They attribute it to the choice of $2,000 as a cutting point so that "the sample sizes in the rationed group are quite small and the sampling errors correspondingly large."

19 *Ibid.*, p. 45. Since the elasticities in Table 5 are not statistically significant, Juster and Shay point out that neither group's elasticity of demand with respect to finance rate changes is large in an absolute sense, but only that the unrationed group's elasticity is relatively larger—more than double that of the rationed group (*ibid.*, p. 32).

A majority of the households in the Consumers Union sample and an even larger proportion of the population are probably in the rationed category. Several factors suggest that there has been a shift of borrowers from the rationed to the unrationed category over the past several decades and that the shift will continue in the future. One is the tendency for lenders to lengthen maturities for the same quality of borrower. The other is the secular growth of incomes and wealth. "On both counts, we may expect consumers to be relatively more responsive to variations in finance rates in the future than at present, and also to be more responsive at present than they had been in earlier decades." [20] As the number of consumers in the unrationed category grows, the greater is the usefulness of finance rates in influencing consumer borrowing decisions on credit contracts of different maturities.

Juster and Shay also find that "responses to rate differences were substantially stronger when finance rates were specified for borrowers than when identical rates of charge were unspecified, although implied by payment details." [21] They note, too, that response to specified finance rates was greater when finance rates are high than when they are low. These responses may have some upward bias. For many respondents believe finance rates to be lower than they are and thus may have rejected high specified rates by mistakenly believing that lower cost alternatives are available to them in the market. [22]

USE OF DEBT VS. LIQUID ASSETS

As noted earlier in this chapter, special problems of rate quotation arise for consumers who have liquid assets at the time they incur debt. To what extent are such consumers willing to use liquid assets as a partial or complete substitute for debt? To what extent would their decisions be affected by a more precise knowledge of finance rates?

---

20 *Ibid.*, p. 46. The authors note the possibility that increased responsiveness could be offset to the extent that consumer wants expand with rising incomes, wealth, and access to credit.

21 *Ibid.*, p. 75.

22 *Ibid.*, p. 75.

Except for demand deposits and cash, liquid assets usually bring in pecuniary income to their owners. Rates of return on income-bearing liquid assets are generally expressed as effective annual interest rates or yields. The compounding intervals used in determining these rates vary according to the nature of the credit or deposit agreement and are, in the main, a quarter, a half year, or a year.

The analysis of Juster and Shay referred to above suggests that consumers with liquid assets of $2,000 and over have a greater elasticity of demand for consumer credit with respect to changes in finance rates than consumers with liquid assets of $2,000 or less.[23] A November 1959 survey of the Survey Research Center provides information on consumer attitudes toward the concurrent holding of liquid assets and debt. A number of consumers were asked their opinions on why a person buys a car on time even though he has sufficient money (savings) in the bank to pay cash. As Table 7 indicates, 68 per cent give what may be termed positive reasons for such behavior: 56 per cent state that he is earmarking his cash for other purposes and 12 per cent state that he is gaining in some way by using the credit. Less than 7 per cent give derogatory reasons for such behavior. In describing such a person, 52 per cent use flattering adjectives such as intelligent and informed and 17 per cent use unflattering adjectives such as stupid and foolish. Thus, on balance, consumers view holding debt and liquid assets concurrently as rational behavior.

In an earlier, essentially deductive treatment of the same problem, Haberler says: "Those who incur instalment debt in spite of the fact that they possess liquid assets must have strong reasons for not using these assets for the purchase of goods. Instalment credit is expensive." [24] He advances the following as possible reasons: (1) consumers may consider liquid assets as long-term assets to be held for long-term purposes; (2) they may lack confidence in their will power to replace any liquid assets which are liquidated; and (3) liquidating liquid assets may involve costs or loss of potential

---

23 *Ibid.*, pp. 36–38.
24 Haberler, *Consumer Instalment Credit,* p. 44.

profit.[25] His first two reasons closely parallel the first two reasons
given in Table 7.

TABLE 7

Consumer Attitudes Toward Credit Users with Liquid Assets

Reasons Given (first question)	Per Cent of Replies	Description (second question)	Per Cent of Replies
To keep bank account for emergencies intact	42	Intelligent; informed; plans ahead	30
Difficulty of replacing savings	5	Cautious; conservative	11
Cash wanted for something else	9	Wise guy; smart; shrewd	11
	56		52
To establish credit	6		
Better service; better price	5		
Use of car while paying	1		
	12		
Only derogatory statements; no reason	7	Stupid; unwise; foolish; crazy	12
		Does not calculate; not good with money; poorly informed	4
		Impatient; impulsive; extravagant	1
			17
Other; don't know; not ascertained	25	Other; average; ordinary; don't know; not ascertained	31
Total	100		100

SOURCE: November 1959 Interim Survey of the Survey Research Center of the
University of Michigan. The questions asked consumers were: "Speaking of buying a car on time, Mr. Smith has just done so although he has enough money
in the bank to pay cash. Why do you think he bought the care on time? What
kind of a man is he?"

Philip Klein's National Bureau study of financial adjustments
to unemployment indicates that the two most frequently used techniques of adjusting financially to unemployment were to decrease
savings and checking accounts (liquid assets) and to borrow money:
40 per cent of the 1,836 households which experienced unemployment over an extended period decreased liquid assets as an adjust-

25 *Ibid.*, pp. 44–45.

TABLE 8

Relation Between Personal Debt and Liquid Assets, by Income Group, Early 1959 [a]

(per cent of spending units)

	All Spending Units	1958 Money Income Before Taxes (dollars)								
		Under 1,000	1,000– 1,999	2,000– 2,999	3,000– 3,999	4,000– 4,999	5,000– 5,999	6,000– 7,499	7,500– 9,999	10,000 and over
No debt	40	58	57	44	36	32	30	29	31	49
No liquid assets	8	27	21	14	5	4	3	1	1	b
Some liquid assets	32	31	36	30	31	28	27	28	30	49
Some debt	60	42	43	56	64	68	70	71	69	51
No liquid assets	17	34	29	30	23	17	11	6	4	2
Some liquid assets	43	7	15	26	41	51	59	65	65	49
Debt as a percentage of liquid assets:										
Under 100	19	4	6	14	17	22	25	27	31	27
100 and over	23	3	9	11	24	30	34	38	34	23
All cases	100	100	100	100	100	100	100	100	100	100

SOURCE: "1959 Survey of Consumer Finances, the Financial Position of Consumers," *Federal Reserve Bulletin*, July 1959, p. 721.

a Personal debt and liquid assets as of time of interview; income before taxes in preceding year. Personal debt includes all short- and intermediate-term consumer debt other than charge accounts and excludes mortgage and business debt. Liquid assets include U.S. savings bonds, checking accounts, savings accounts in banks, and shares in savings and loan associations and credit unions; currency is excluded.

b No cases reported or less than .05 per cent.

NOTE: Detail may not add to total because of rounding.

ment technique and 26 per cent borrowed money.[26] This indicates
that liquid assets are important in maintaining consumption and
credit standing in an emergency such as unemployment. This liquidity value possessed by liquid assets (mentioned by 42 per cent
of the replies in Table 7) may well compensate, in the minds of
many persons, for a substantial difference between the earnings rate
on liquid assets and the finance rate on credit.

The Survey Research Center data provide no direct evidence on
the extent to which consumers might use liquid assets as a partial
or full substitute for instalment debt if they knew finance rates.
Indirect evidence is inconclusive but may be mentioned to give
some perspective on the practical importance of the problem. Table
8 shows that, in early 1959, 43 per cent of all spending units sur-
veyed had both personal debt and liquid assets: 19 per cent had
liquid assets in excess of personal debt and 23 per cent had liquid-
asset holdings which were less than their personal debt. Further-
more, those with liquid assets in excess of debt were relatively numerous in all but the lowest income groups. These facts mean that
(1) roughly one-third of spending units with debt could have eliminated their entire personal debt had they chosen to substitute liquid assets for debt, (2) an additional one-third of those spending
units with debt could have reduced their debt by substituting liquid
assets, and (3) liquidation of debt could have been distributed
widely among income groups.

Tables 8 and 9 give some support to the inference that the dollar
decrease in personal debt would have been substantial if all spending
units with personal debt and liquid assets in early 1959 had sub-
stituted assets for debt. The top four income groups contained (1)
44 per cent of all spending units (Table 9), (2) the highest percentages of spending units with personal debt (Table 8), (3) the highest
percentages (25 per cent or more) of spending units with liquid assets in excess of personal debt (Table 8), (4) the highest percentages
of spending units with personal debt of $200 and over (Table 9),
and (5) the highest percentages of spending units with liquid assets

26 Philip A. Klein, *Financial Adjustments to Unemployment,* NBER Occasional Paper 93, New York, 1965, Table 6.

TABLE 9

Distribution of Personal Debt and Liquid Assets, by Income Group, Early 1959 [a]

(per cent of spending units)

	All Spending Units	1958 Money Income Before Taxes (dollars)								
		Under 1,000	1,000– 1,999	2,000– 2,999	3,000– 3,999	4,000– 4,999	5,000– 5,999	6,000– 7,499	7,500– 9,999	10,000 and over
Amount of personal debt										
Under $100	10	19	14	12	11	14	9	5	5	5
$100–$199	7	9	10	11	7	6	8	7	4	3
$200 and over	43	14	20	33	46	47	53	59	59	43
All cases with debt	60	42	43	56	64	68	70	71	69	51
Amount of liquid assets										
Zero	25	61	50	44	28	21	14	7	4	2
$1–$199	18	8	14	15	25	28	26	24	13	4
$200 and over	57	30	36	41	47	52	60	70	83	94
All cases	100	100	100	100	100	100	100	100	100	100
Spending units in each income group	100	7	13	12	12	12	12	12	12	8

Source: "1959 Survey of Consumer Finances, the Financial Position of Consumers," *Federal Reserve Bulletin*, July 1959, pp. 713, 715, and 721.

[a] See Table 8.

Note: Detail may not add to total because of rounding.

of $200 and over (Table 9).[27] A considerable number of the spending units in each of the four top income groups had both debt and liquid assets in excess of $200, for the combined percentages exceed 100, successively, as follows: 113, 129, 142, 137 (Table 9).

Since a substantial proportion of debt owed by spending units with liquid assets appears to be in the income groups of $5,000 and over, increased knowledge of finance rates would have the greatest chance of influencing a substitution of liquid assets for debt to the extent that an upward revision of their credit cost estimate made it appear desirable to hold fewer liquid assets and borrow less. Yet it is important to know both the absolute number as well as the proportion of borrowers with incomes above $5,000 who are misinformed. All borrowers have the option of not making a given purchase when costs appear to be higher. Borrowers with liquid assets have the additional option of borrowing less and still making the purchase.

Unfortunately, our data do not permit even an approximate estimate of the number of consumers who may be misinformed. Table 10 does, however, shed some light on the problem, for it shows that, when asked what interest or carrying charges one has to pay for buying a car on time, 40 to 48 per cent of the spending units in income groups of $5,000 and over gave answers which led to computed effective annual rates under 7 per cent. Spending units in these income groups contained about 29 per cent of all spending units with personal debt and about 27 per cent of all spending units with both personal debt and liquid assets in 1959.[28] Only 5

27 The $10,000 and over group is an exception in points (2) and (4).
28 These percentages are computed from Tables 8 and 9 as follows:

Percentage of Spending Units in Each Group with

Income Group (dollars)	% of All Spending Units (1)	Personal Debt (2)	Personal Debt & Liquid Assets (3)	Cols. 1 × 2 (4)	Cols. 1 × 3 (5)
5,000–5,999	12	70	59	8.4	7.1
6,000–7,499	12	71	65	8.5	7.8
7,500–9,999	12	69	65	8.3	7.8
10,000 and over	8	49	49	4.1	3.9
Percentage of all spending units with:					
Personal debt				29.3	
Personal debt and liquid assets					26.6

TABLE 10

Cumulative Percentage Distribution of Consumer Estimates of Finance Rates on Auto Financing, 1959, by Selected Income Groups, and New-Car Instalment Financing Rates, 1954–55 and 1959

Annual Rate (per cent)	Distribution of Consumer Responses by Income Groups[a] (dollars)			Effective Annual New-Car Finance Rate[b] (per cent)	New-Car Financing Instalment Rates[c] (number of contracts)			
	5,000–7,499	7,500–9,999	10,000 and over		All Credit Sources, 1954–55	Banks,[d] 1954–55	Sales Finance Companies, 1954–55	Large Sales Finance Companies, 1959
Under 4	4	1	1	Under 5	1	2	1	0
Under 7	40	48	45	Under 7	5	8	2	0
Under 10	54	64	60	Under 9	20	30	11	0
Under 13	73	85	80	Under 13	88	92	85	65
Under 16	80	87	84	Under 15	96	97	95	96
All rates	100	100	100	All rates	100	100	100	100

a Obtained from November 1959 Interim Survey of the Survey Research Center of the University of Michigan. The question asked consumers was: "Do you happen to know how much interest or carrying charges one has to pay to buy a car on time; suppose you need a thousand dollars which you would repay monthly over 2 years; about how much do you think the interest or carrying charges would be each year?" Then percentages are based on usable responses. Nonusable responses (don't know,

uncodable answer, or answer not ascertained) comprised the following percentages of total responses in the three income groups reading from left to right: 28, 19, 32.

b Computed by the constant ratio formula.

c 1954–55 rates are based on data compiled by the Federal Reserve System. 1959 rates are computed by the National Bureau.

d Includes direct and indirect financing.

per cent of new-car instalment contracts were financed at effective annual rates of 6 per cent or less in 1954–55. Judging solely from the large sales finance company's figures in Table 10, an even lower percentage of new-car contracts were probably financed at rates of under 7 per cent in 1959.

Interpretation of the responses in Table 10 as effective annual rates lends support to the inference that a not inconsiderable number of spending units with both liquid assets and personal debt have some misconception of the finance rates they are paying. Interpretation of the responses in Table 10 as computational annual rates does not lend support to such an inference. Unfortunately, there is no way to choose between the two interpretations, for the survey did not ascertain which interpretation respondents had in mind in giving their answers.

Yet even if it were possible to measure the number of persons who were misinformed about finance rates, the crucial questions of the effects of acquiring accurate information would remain. How urgent are the purchases which might be foregone if consumers' estimates of credit cost rise? How many persons would find that knowledge of finance rates would cause them to liquidate assets and curtail borrowing?

The evidence reviewed supports the general notion that a number of people use instalment buying as a budgetary device. Many consumers feel that they lack the necessary fortitude to save ahead and buy for cash and that instalment buying gives them better discipline in handling finances. It is likely that many consumers place a high value on keeping liquid assets intact for other purposes; finance rate information might merely provide a simple way to measure the relative costs when borrowing rates are made comparable to rates paid for savings.

4. Procedures and Problems in Converting Existing Finance Charge Information to Comparable Forms

CONSUMERS WHO WISH TO COMPARE different types of finance charge information can do so by converting them to a comparable form. This chapter is concerned with the procedures and problems of conversion. Computational rates or equivalents are the usual starting point in any conversion precedure, for finance charges in consumer financing are universally computed by multiplying such rates or equivalents by either the amount borrowed or the amount of credit outstanding.

Converting Computational Rates (Equivalents) to Dollar Charges and to Monthly Payments

The procedures for converting add-on, discount, and per cent per month rates (or equivalents) to dollar finance charges are described in Chapter 2. On instalment contracts on which monthly payments are uniform in amount, the size of each monthly payment is determined by adding the amount borrowed to the finance charge and dividing the sum by the number of monthly payments. On instalment contracts in which monthly payments are not uniform, the size of each monthly payment must be determined individually in accordance with the details of the contract.

Converting One Form of Computational Rate (Equivalent) to Another

Converting one form of computational rate (equivalent) to another form, e.g., add-on to discount, requires computing effective monthly or annual rates as a step in the process. Similarly, converting dollar finance charges to a computational rate (equivalent)—other than the one used to obtain the charges—requires computing monthly or annual finance rates as a step in the process.

Effective rates occupy a strategic role in both of the above conversions and are the end product in the conversion of computational rates (equivalents) or dollar charges to effective rates. Since the procedures and problems are similar in all of these conversions, they are covered for all three in the section which follows.

Converting Computational Rates (Equivalents) or Dollar Charges to Monthly and Annual Finance Rates

CHOICE AND USE OF FORMULAS

With one exception, conversion of computational rates (equivalents) and dollar charges to effective rates requires the use of formulas or tables based on formulas. The exception is a flat per cent per month rate since it is both a computational rate and an effective monthly (*not* an annual) rate.

Among the available formulas, six are referred to most frequently.[1] They are:

Name Used in This Study	Alternate Names	Symbol Used in This Study Monthly Rate	Annual Rate
1. Annuity or actuarial formula with a monthly base	Present Worth formula	k	y_m
2. Annuity or actuarial formula with a yearly base	Actuarial yield formula, small-loan method formula	k	y_a
3. Constant ratio formula	Uniform method formula	k_c	y_c
4. Direct ratio formula	Pro-rata method formula	k_d	y_d
5. Minimum yield formula	Priority method formula		
6. Maximum yield formula	Residuary method formula		

[1] For derivation of all six formulas, see Milan V. Ayres, *Instalment Mathe-*

Formulas (5) and (6) are disregarded because they are based on rather unrealistic assumptions requiring the allocation of the entire finance charge to either the beginning instalment payments (minimum yield) or to the ending payment (maximum yield). This leaves three formulas for effective monthly rates and four for effective annual rates. There is one less for effective monthly rates because formulas (1) and (2) give the same result for monthly but not for annual rates.

Formulas (2), (3), and (4) give annual rates that are twelve times their respective monthly rates. This means that the relationship among annual rates and among monthly rates under the three formulas is the same. For convenience in exposition, this relationship is discussed in terms of annual rates, but it applies equally to monthly rates.

Chart 1 indicates that the y_m formula gives the highest effective annual rates, the y_a and y_d formulas the lowest rates, and the y_c formula in-between rates. The y_d rates are not shown on the chart but can be approximated from it, for they are virtually the same as y_a rates.

As explained in Appendix A, under existing computational methods in consumer finance, the y_m and y_a formulas are two ways of measuring yields just as inches and meters are two ways of measuring distance. Both are theoretically defensible and there is no "scientific" way of choosing between them. The y_d formula is somewhat less complicated than the y_a formula and gives similar results. As can be seen from Chart 1, the y_c formula gives a different maturity pattern of effective rates from the y_m, y_a, and y_d formulas. Simplicity of computation is its main advantage over the other three.[2]

Any one of the four formulas would serve as a self-contained sys-

---

matics Handbook, New York, 1946, Chaps. 25–30. For derivation of formulas (2) through (6), see M. R. Neifeld, Neifeld's Guide to Instalment Computation, Easton, 1954, Chaps. 7–11. For a comparison of formulas (2), (3), (4), and (6), see H. E. Stelson, "The Rate of Interest in Instalment Payment Plans," The American Mathematical Monthly, April 1949, pp. 257–261.

2 H. E. Stelson has developed a formula which, in ease of computation and results, is similar to the constant ratio formula. This formula, designated as $r\beta$ in the article cited below, gives results which are slightly lower (about .1 per cent) than those of the constant ratio formula. See H. E. Stelson, "The Rate of Interest on Instalment Payment Loans," The American Mathematical Monthly, May 1953, pp. 326–329.

CHART 1

Comparable Effective Annual Finance Rates for
Monthly Payment Contracts with 6, 7, and 8 Per Cent
Annual Add-On and Discount Rates,
by Maturity

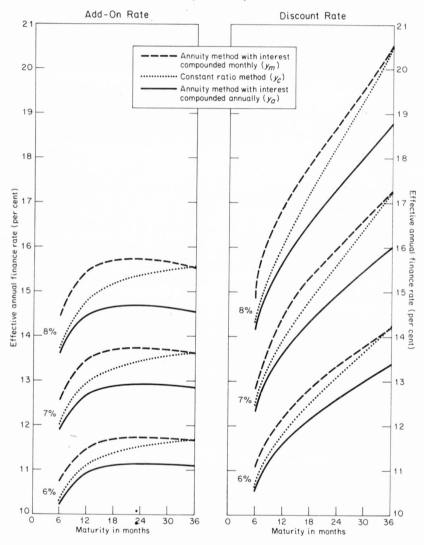

Source: Tables B-1 and B-2.

tem in comparing rates on different instalment contracts. Any one of the four would also probably serve as a yardstick if used by consumers to determine whether to use liquid assets instead of credit. It is true, of course, that yields on liquid assets are usually expressed in terms of an annuity formula using quarterly or semiannual compounding rather than monthly or annual compounding. The spread between liquid-asset yields and finance rates is so great, however, that any consumers who might be interested in making a comparison would probably reach about the same conclusions, whether they compared liquid-asset yield with y_a, y_d, y_e, or y_m finance rates. Thus, if a liquid-asset yield is 4 or 5 per cent and finance rates by the four formulas are successively 14.4, 14.4, 14.8, and 15.5 per cent, the differences between liquid-assets yields and finance rates are so great with all four formulas that they overshadow the difference in the spread from one formula to the next. Scientific accuracy is hardly a realistic goal for comparison under the circumstances.

Monthly finance rates would have to be multiplied by twelve by consumers for comparison with liquid-asset yields. The comparison is thus somewhat more complex than the comparison between annual rates and liquid-asset yields.

In order to investigate the views of regulatory authorities on technical aspects of the various methods of converting existing finance charge information to comparable forms, questionnaires were sent out to eighty state supervisors responsible for the administration and enforcement of laws governing consumer credit agencies. Forty-five replies were received. Because two respondents requested that their answers not be published in any form, the results reported are based upon forty-three replies covering thirty-four states.

The state supervisor survey asked: What method of determining this (effective) rate do you prefer? Thirty of the forty-three who returned the questionnaire answered as follows:

Method of Determining Effective Rate	Number Who Prefer This Method
Constant ratio formula	14
Annuity or actuarial formula [3]	13[4]
Direct ratio formula	2[4]
Per cent per month	2

[3] No attempt was made in the survey to distinguish between the y_a and y_m annuity or actuarial formulas.

[4] One supervisor gave the direct ratio formula as an alternative to the annuity formula and is counted twice.

The answers indicate that persons have different formula preferences and help explain why different people get different finance
rate answers to the same problem. The state supervisor survey also
investigated whether the personnel of financing agencies could convert financing charges to effective annual rates with or without the
use of rate tables based upon some formula. The results are discussed in Appendix C.

RELEVANCE OF EX ANTE COMPUTATIONS

Consumers who wish to compute effective rates may be in a position
to compute them either *ex ante* (foresight) or *ex post* (hind-
sight). An *ex ante* effective rate is computed at the time the credit
is extended and requires the following information: amount of
credit extended, finance charge in dollars, and scheduled payment
dates and amounts throughout the credit period. It can be computed on virtually all consumer credit transactions on which a
separate finance charge is made. Indeed, a number of hypothetical
ex ante rates can be estimated on any credit transaction at the start
of the credit period, each one depending on a hypothetical schedule
of payment amounts and dates.

An *ex post* effective rate requires the following information:
amount of credit extended, finance charge in dollars, and actual
payment dates and amounts during the credit period. Clearly, an
accurate estimate of an *ex post* rate can be made only after a credit
contract is fulfilled since many are not paid on schedule.

The *ex ante* and *ex post* bases serve different purposes and which
one is used depends on whether an effective rate is desired to facilitate a rational choice for a given transaction or to reveal the cost
of a completed transaction in order to facilitate a choice on future
credit transaction. It is important to consider relevant problems
with this distinction in mind.

When a consumer shops to buy a washing machine on credit,
what matters for the purpose of comparing alternative current rates
of charge and liquid-asset yields is the predetermined (*ex ante*)
effective rate on the assumption the contract will be paid on schedule. The consumer may have an *ex post* rate on a previous credit
purchase of a washing machine or analogous good. This rate will

be of help in shopping for a new credit purchase only if finance rates have not changed or have all changed proportionately between purchase dates *and* if the consumer pays off the new contract on the same schedule as he paid off the previous contract.

Business firms constantly face situations which are analogous to those faced by consumer credit users. When a corporation floats a bond issue, it sets the prospective yield in line with yields on comparable existing bonds on the assumption that the whole issue will be redeemed at par at maturity. This is an *ex ante* yield. The issue may have, as many issues do, a call provision permitting the corportion to retire bonds at varying times before maturity at varying call prices. A whole series of hypothetical *ex ante* yields can be worked out before the bond is issued, each based on a different pattern of redemptions. Only one actual *ex post* yield will eventuate, however, and this can be known only after the last bond is retired.

GRADUATED RATE CONTRACTS

A number of small-loan laws and a few instalment and industrial loan laws have two, three, or four graduated rates. Consumers who wish to determine *ex ante* effective rates on graduated rate contracts can do so by special manipulation of a formula or by a trial and error procedure which gives approximately similar results.[5]

The special manipulation may be illustrated by applying an annuity formula to a graduated instalment contract using the ceiling monthly rates in Massachusetts' small-loan law, viz.: $2\frac{1}{2}$ per cent on the part of a loan under $200; 2 per cent on the part from $200 to $600; $1\frac{3}{4}$ per cent on the part from $600 to $1,000; and $\frac{3}{4}$ per cent on the part over $1,000. Any loan over $200 is regarded as several loans, each at its respective rate. Thus a $600 loan for twelve months is regarded as a $200 loan at $2\frac{1}{2}$ per cent and a $400 loan at at 2 per cent. Principal payment on the $200 loan is deferred and only interest is collected until the $400 loan at 2 per cent is paid off. Tables based on ordinary annuity formulas at the respective monthly rates give the interest in dollars and the principal outstanding at the end of each month. Dividing the sum of monthly

---

[5] For an explanation of the trial and error procedure, see Ayres, *Instalment Mathematics*, pp. 206–208.

interest charges by the sum of the principal amounts outstanding at the end of each month gives the effective *ex ante* monthly rate over the life of the contract.[6] Examples of maximum effective *ex ante* rates on twelve-month loans of selected sizes under Massachusetts' small-loan law are as follows (in per cent):

Size of Loan (dollars)	Monthly (k formula)	Annual (y_a formula)
100	2.50	30.00
300	2.42	29.04
500	2.29	27.48
1,000	2.12	25.44
1,500	1.87	22.44

Each such rate is the effective rate a borrower incurs throughout the whole loan period if: (1) he borrows on a twelve-month basis; (2) he repays the loan in twelve equal monthly payments as scheduled; and (3) the principal part of each payment is applied entirely to the portion of the loan at the lowest rate until that portion is paid off and then applied to each succeeding part in a similar manner. An effective rate computed under this interpretation is an *ex ante* rate.

An alternative interpretation assumes that the loan mix changes each month and that, as a consequence, the effective rate also changes each month. This interpretation, in effect, assumes that the borrower negotiates a new loan each month at zero refinancing expense. The series of rates so computed (twelve on a twelve-month loan, twenty-four on a twenty-four-month loan, and so on) are also *ex ante* rates.

TREATMENT OF RECORDING AND FILING FEES

Financing agencies and sellers pay recording and filing fees to public officials for some secured instalment credit transactions. Some small-loan laws require lenders to absorb the fees in the finance charge. The remaining small-loan laws and most other types of con-

[6] A similar procedure is necessary to determine the flat monthly payment on loans under a graduated rate structure. Specialized publishers have been preparing flat monthly payment schedules and selling them to consumer finance companies since graduated structures first appeared in the middle 1930's.

sumer financing laws permit creditors to charge consumers extra for such fees either on all credit transactions or only on those credit transactions above a specified minimum size.

Any fees which are passed on to consumers can, of course, be added to the finance charge which is used to compute an effective rate. Practically speaking, such fees can probably be ignored. They are too small to affect the usefulness of an effective rate as a comparative yardstick. They are not included in computing mortgage rates even though they are much more common in mortgages than in consumer finance. Because they are small, their inclusion in the finance charge results in uneven add-on, discount, and per cent per month rates, e.g., an add-on rate of 6.003 per cent, and complicates the use of effective rate tables or charts based on computational rates.

TREATMENT OF MINIMUM CHARGES

Most retail instalment financing laws specify minimum charges ranging from $10 to $25 on automobile financing and a fair number specify minimum charges from $5 to $20 on other retail instalment financing. Minimum charges are less frequent in cash loan laws and are also smaller, ranging for the most part from $1 to $3 and, in a few cases, from $10 to $15. Any of the four formulas can be used to compute effective rates in minimum charge contracts. Such rates are likely to be relatively high because the minimum charge is used only when it exceeds what the regular charge would have been. Where such rates are high because the contract involves a relatively small amount of debt or has a short maturity, they may need to be supplemented by dollar charge information to place credit cost in proper perspective.

SPECIAL FINANCING PLANS

Special financing plans may or may not require special techniques for determining effective rates. The problem is discussed here in connection with each of four such plans.

Irregular Payment Contracts. Two types of irregularities need to be distinguished. The first type, which occurs in many instalment contracts, involves deferring the first payment beyond a month to obtain convenient payment dates. Thus, if a consumer buys a car on the instalment plan on May 5, the first payment may be scheduled for June 15 or July 1 instead of June 5.

While the four formulas already described are devised for contracts in which the payments are equal and evenly spaced, they can also be applied to contracts which have only slight deferments of the first payment. Such irregularities have relatively little effect on the effective rate, except on short-term, higher-rate contracts.[7] Longer deferments of the first payment would require special formulas in order to compute effective rates.

A second type of irregularity occurs in contracts which have several irregular payments or a last payment which is markedly higher than preceding ones, the so-called balloon payment. Instalment loans to teachers, for example, sometimes call for regular payments during the school year and no payments during the summer vacation period. Because of legislative restrictions and lender interest in encouraging regular payments, only a small minority of instalment contracts have irregular payments of this second type. Special formulas are required to determine effective rates on such contracts.[8]

Add-On Instalment Contracts. These are contracts which cover successive instalment purchases by a given buyer from a given seller. As each purchase is made, the amount owed on it is added to the

---

[7] The effect of a deferred first payment without added charges is to reduce the effective rate. The extent of the reduction depends on the level of the computational rate and the length of the deferment period. The following tabulation makes it possible to compare the extent to which effective monthly finance rates are reduced when the first payment is deferred fifteen or thirty days beyond the regular (thirty-day) first-payment period.

Maturity (months)	Annual Add-On Rate	*Effective Monthly Rate (in per cent) When Timing of First Payment Is:*		
		Regular	+15 days	+30 days
12	6%	0.908	0.845	0.785
	15	2.219	2.050	1.866
24	6	0.927	0.890	0.857
	15	2.215	2.122	2.036
36	6	0.923	0.898	0.874
	15	2.165	2.112	2.039

The writer is indebted to his colleague Earl K. Bowen for deriving the formula $[P\,(1+ku)=R \times a_{v_k}]$ for computing the irregular-payment contract rates. In this formula, in which k must be found by trial and error, P = the amount financed, k = the effective monthly rate, u = the fraction of a month's deferment in the first payment, R = the monthly payment, v = the number of monthly payments, and a_{v_k} = the present value of an annuity of 1 per annum at k.

[8] For such formulas, see Ayres, *Instalment Mathematics*, pp. 134–135, and *Neifeld's Guide*, pp. 203–214.

contract covering previous purchases. When successive purchases are added and no adjustment is made for amounts owed on previous purchases, an *ex ante* effective rate can be computed on each purchase separately as if each purchase were put into a separate instalment contract. In some cases an existing instalment contract is canceled when a new instalment purchase is made and the purchase and the balance of the old contract are added in a new contract. The finance charge adjustment needed to compute a new *ex ante* effective rate by one of the formulas is the charge on the new contract less any prepayment refund on the old contract.[9] Some retail instalment financing laws prohibit add-on contracts.

Retailer Revolving Credit Plans. There are special problems in the computation of an *ex ante* effective rate on revolving credit transactions. If a customer buys goods in a given month and pays for them during that month, the purchases are customarily treated as charge-account purchases and no separate finance charge is levied. Analogously, if a customer buys goods during a month but pays for them in a succeeding month or months, no separate finance charge is made in the month of purchase. Any finance cost for that month is, as with charge account credit, included in the price of the goods.

To take a specific example, assume that a store's billing date is the first of each month and that a customer buys $300 in merchandise at various times during January and makes no payments in January. Any credit cost for January is included in the merchandise price of $300. There is no separate finance or revolving credit charge in January.

There is, however, a revolving charge on February 1 on the $300 which the customer owes. At a rate of $1\frac{1}{2}$ per cent a month, the revolving credit charge is $4.50 and the total owed is $304.50. According to some observers, the effective rate cannot be determined on February 1 because it depends on the customer's payment pattern in the future.[10] This is true *ex post* but not *ex ante*. As far as

[9] See Appendix D for a discussion of the nature of prepayment refunds, refinancing, extension, and delinquency charges and their relation to finance charge computation and quotation.

[10] See, for example, *Consumer Credit Labeling Bill,* Hearings before a Subcommittee of the Committee on Banking and Currency, U.S. Senate, 86th Congress, 2nd Session, Washington, 1960, p. 364; and Robert W. Johnson, *Methods of Stating Finance Charges,* Columbia University, New York, 1961, p. 97.

the customer is concerned, he is paying $4.50 to use $300 for one month. This is an *ex ante* effective monthly rate of $1\frac{1}{2}$ per cent (k, k_c, and k_d) and effective annual rates of 18 per cent (y_a y_c, and y_d) and 19.56 per cent (y_m).[11] Comparison of effective rates of different sellers computed by one of these formulas is important to the customer if he wishes to shop for the lowest revolving credit charge in order to get the best credit bargain.

It is true that, once the customer incurs the revolving credit of $300, his *ex post* effective rate goes up if he makes any payment before March 1, because he repays in advance of the scheduled date. But this is unimportant to the customer when he is shopping for the best credit bargain. In any practical sense, it is also unimportant in deciding on his payment pattern once the revolving credit charge has been incurred.

Bank Check-Credit Plans. A number of banks have these plans and several states have special laws governing such plans. In the typical plan a bank provides a borrower with a number of checks which may be drawn up to a maximum outstanding balance. The borrower cashes these checks as he needs money and repays every month some fraction of either the maximum or the outstanding balance. Interest is charged, usually at the rate of 1 or $1\frac{1}{2}$ per cent a month on the unpaid balance, from the time each check is cashed or from the time each check clears the bank. In addition, the borrower pays a service charge of so much a check, usually 25 cents, each time he cashes a check. The total finance charge is the interest on the unpaid balance plus the service charge.

For these plans a consumer cannot compute an effective *ex ante* rate at the time he gets the checks unless he knows the dates on which he will cash the checks and the amount to be cashed on each date. He does know, however, that the effective *ex ante* monthly rate will be in excess of the specified per month rate on the unpaid balance. The amount of the excess depends on (1) the size of the service charge per check, (2) the dollar amount of the checks cashed on any date, and (3) the dates of the month they are cashed. The

---

11 The principle remains the same but the computation becomes somewhat more complex in revolving credit transactions which involve graduated rates, e.g., $1\frac{1}{2}$ per cent a month on the first $500 owed and 1 per cent a month on any part of the balance owed above $500.

amount of the excess will be smaller the smaller is the service charge, the larger is the amount of the checks cashed on any day, and the earlier in the month is the day on which the check is cashed.

As an illustration, the following tabulation gives estimated effective *ex ante* monthly rates (in per cent) using a 1 per cent per month rate on the unpaid balance, a thirty-day month, service charges of 10 and 25 cents per check, the first and last days of the month as check-cashing dates, and $100 and $1,000 checks.

	$100 Check		$1,000 Check	
Day of Month on Which Check Is Cashed	Service Charge of 10¢ Per Check	Service Charge of 25¢ Per Check	Service Charge of 10¢ Per Check	Service Charge of 25¢ Per Check
First day	1.10	1.25	1.01	1.03
Thirtieth day	4.00	8.50	1.30	1.75

MEANINGFULNESS OF RETAIL INSTALMENT FINANCE RATES

When sellers extend credit they have a choice between setting one price for the goods and credit combined and setting separate prices for the goods and credit. Sellers, in fact, follow both policies now. Some—for instance, instalment jewelers and department stores for open-account credit—generally set one price and others—for instance, automobile and appliance dealers—generally set separate prices. Retail instalment financing laws recognize the right of the seller to choose, for they set ceiling finance charges, but they do not specify any minimum charge below which a seller cannot go.

What counts to sellers and buyers is the total price (cost) of the goods and credit combined, whether expressed as one price or as separate prices. Sellers who set separate goods and credit prices can use varying combinations to achieve any given total price.

Data supplied by the National Automobile Dealers Association measuring the relation between automobile dealers' average operating profit and average finance reserve on new cars and trucks imply that some shifting of goods price to credit price occurred between 1950 and 1959. Table 11 indicates that per unit average operating profit (including average finance reserve) dropped sharply from 1950 through 1954 and remained at a generally lower level

TABLE 11

Relation of Average Operating Profit and Average Finance
Reserve Per New Car Unit, 1950–59

Year	Average Operating Profit (Including Finance Reserve)	Average Finance Reserve[a]	Average Finance Reserve as a Percentage of Average Operating Profit
1950	208	n.a.	
1951	201	n.a.	
1952	175	n.a.	
1953	100	n.a.	
1954	29	26.60	91.7
1955	80	36.54	45.7
1956	39	45.44	116.5
1957	35	48.13	137.5
1958	11	48.39	439.9
1959	70	50.06	71.5

SOURCE: National Automobile Dealers Association. 1949 is the first year for which data are available.

a The average finance reserve covers the reserves on both new and used units but, according to the NADA method of reporting, is related to new units only.

from 1955 through 1959. It also indicates that the per unit average finance reserve increased substantially between 1954 (the first year for which figures are available) and 1959. In three of these six years, the average finance reserve exceeded the average operating profit, i.e., the average operating profit excluding the average finance reserve was negative.

Since it is the total goods-credit price which counts and since sellers who have separate goods and credit prices can vary them to obtain a given total, the question arises of the meaningfulness of any separate goods or credit price.[12] If a consumer determines the finance rate on any pending instalment purchase, does such a rate have any meaning or usefulness?

To hold that any finance rate does not convey the cost of credit requires setting up standards by which finance rates accurately represent such costs. Whenever a seller has separate prices on joint sales, consumers may respond differently to alternative price com-

12 See, for example, *Consumer Credit Labeling Bill*, pp. 305 and 406, and Johnson, *Finance Charges*, pp. 93–97.

binations. When the credit transaction is separate from the sale of the good, as in direct lending, the finance rate must reveal the credit cost. If sellers raised finance rates and lowered goods prices to increase joint sales, people might gravitate to direct lenders. If sellers lowered finance rates and raised goods prices, consumers might seek lower-cost goods sellers. Under these conditions, separately stated prices help determine the combined market cost to the consumer on joint sales. Each price conveys to consumers its market share of the total cost of credit purchases.

Legislation reflects this view of the usefulness of separate goods and credit prices to consumers. Retail instalment financing laws universally require instalment sellers to show separate goods and credit prices in dollars. (The credit price is given as zero if no separate charge is made for it.) The Automobile Information Disclosure Act, effective October 1, 1958, requires the posting of the factory-recommended price of a new automobile plus accessories.

CONVERTING FINANCE CHARGES TO RATES
COMPARABLE WITH USURY CEILINGS

As indicated in Chapter 2, forty-seven states and the District of Columbia have usury ceilings which, with the exception of Rhode Island's 30 per cent, vary from 6 to 12 per cent. Courts have generally held that usury ceilings are to be interpreted as effective annual rates, to relate to all costs of a financing transaction rather than only to the "pure interest" cost, and to apply to all financing transactions not specifically exempted by statue or common law.

Consumers who accurately compute finance (i.e., effective annual) rates in the forty-seven states with 6 to 12 per cent usury ceilings will find that many, if not most, of these finance rates exceed the usury ceilings. To prevent possible misunderstanding, consumers should know what costs to include in computing finance rates and when finance rates that exceed usury ceilings are legal and when they are not.

What Costs to Include. In the theoretical works that offer an explanation of why interest exists and analyze the factors determining the level of the interest rate, economists have traditionally been concerned primarily with pure interest cost and have assumed away or ignored service and risk costs. This is illustrated by the following quotation: [13]

> While any exact and practical definition of a pure rate of interest is impossible, we may say roughly that the pure rate is the rate on loans which are practically devoid of chance. . . . In this book, I shall usually confine the concept of the rate of interest to the rate in a (humanly speaking) safe loan, or other contract implying specific sums payable at one date or set of dates in consideration of repayment at another date or set of dates. The essentials in this concept are: (1) definite and assured payments, (2) definite and assured repayments, and (3) definite dates.

The pure interest concept has been applied to the consumer instalment credit market by one writer as follows: [14]

> The interest rate could be regarded as the sole price factor only if the instalment credit had a perfect market such as is assumed in a large part of the general theory of money and credit. If there existed a generally accessible instalment loan market where demand for all types of instalment credit could be satisfied on the same contract terms, at least within certain limits, and consumers could freely renew and extend loans, the price of instalment credit could be thought of unequivocally as interest on the average unpaid balance.

If interest is construed as the pure cost of money alone, there should theoretically be little or no difference among the interest costs of all kinds of loans, for money is a homogeneous commodity and the money markets are highly competitive. The theory has not been tested empirically since measurement of pure interest has not been possible because of the lack of a riskless commodity whose scheduled repayment is certain.

In the absence of a consensus on what constitutes pure interest and, consequently, on how it can be measured, one authority suggests that: [15]

> . . . economists have gradually come to recognize that the interest problem is essentially a numerical problem and should be approached as such. . . . The concept of "pure" or "riskless" interest is metaphysical. The prac-

---

13 Irving Fisher, *The Theory of Interest*, New York, 1954, pp. 34–35.
14 Gottfried Haberler, *Consumer Instalment Credit and Economic Fluctuations*, New York, NBER, 1942, p. 89.
15 Frederick Macauley, *Some Theoretical Problems Suggested by the Movement of Interest Rates, Bond Yields and Stock Prices in the United States Since 1896*, New York, NBER, 1938, pp. 6 and 38.

tical contrast is not between "pure" and "impure" but between "promised" or "expected" and "actual" or "realized." It is quite quixotic to attempt to divide the "promised" (or even "realized") return from a bond into "interest" and "profits" or something else. Moreover, such a division is unnecessary for either theoretical or historical treatment. Bonds and other interest-bearing obligations may be classified according to their ("promised") yields without deciding what the rate of "riskless" yield would be.

In an empirical sense, the term interest rate measures the total annual cost of a credit transaction regardless of the nature of that cost or of the number of components into which the cost may be divided. Three kinds of cost are common to all types of credit transactions, including consumer credit: service, risk, and pure interest. The relative importance of each of these cost elements varies widely among credit transactions. In general, the greater the credit strength of the borrower, the greater is the share of pure interest in total cost and the smaller is the share of risk and service in total cost. To illustrate, pure interest is the major cost while service and risk are negligible costs in lending money on short term to the United States government by buying Treasury bills. Service and risk are the dominant costs and pure interest is a minor cost on a loan to a struggling small business firm and on most consumer credit transactions. Some observers have objected to expressing the finance charge as an effective rate because pure interest is only a small part of the cost of most consumer credit transactions and because they interpret "interest rate" as "pure interest costs." [16]

The term interest rate (or its equivalent, yield) is used in an empirical sense in business, government, and mortgage financing. It generally represents the total annual cost expressed as an effective annual rate on loans, bonds, and other forms of debt, from the very high-grade (in which pure interest cost dominates) to the very low-grade (in which service and risk costs dominate). An interest or finance rate can be used in the same empirical sense in consumer financing.

Courts have generally interpreted the term interest in the empirical rather than the pure interest sense. Their objective has been to prevent lenders from evading usury ceilings by charging

[16] For an example, see the statement of Theodore Beckman in *Consumer Credit Labeling Bill*, p. 333.

pure interest up to the ceiling and then adding one or more extra charges to cover service and risk costs. Most of the special laws governing consumer financing set one ceiling covering all three cost elements. Included here are virtually all retail instalment financing laws, revolving credit laws, small-loan laws, and credit union laws, two-thirds of the instalment loan laws, and one-fourth of the industrial loan laws. Only a minority of special consumer financing laws have separate ceilings for different cost elements. These laws usually contain two ceilings, one to cover pure interest and risk and the other to cover service costs.[17] Both the one-charge and two-charge laws usually permit creditors to charge consumers separately for any filing or recording fees which creditors pay public officials for a credit transaction.

Measurement of total cost rather than pure interest is the relevant magnitude to consumers whether the measure is in dollar or rate form. In seeking the lowest cost alternative, the consumer wants the charge or rate which is necessary to cover his credit risk and to provide the desired credit service.

Legality of Finance Charges Which Exceed Usury Ceilings. Whether finance charges may legally exceed usury ceilings depends on (1) the existence of usury ceilings, (2) state court interpretations of the scope of credit transactions which are construed as usury, and (3) the existence of legislation permitting higher rates of charge on the extension of credit to individuals.

State courts have adhered to the time-price doctrine and exempted retail instalment financing from the usury laws in all states other than Arkansas (since 1952). Except for that state, retail instalment finance charges are legally subject either to ceilings in retail instalment financing laws or to no ceiling in the absence of such a law.[18] In Arkansas retail instalment finance charges are subject to the usury ceilings.

Cash loans are subject to usury laws unless specifically exempted

---

17 For advocacy of a three-charge system, see Roland A. Baker, "Statutory Limitations on Small Loan Charges," *Personal Finance Law Quarterly Report,* fall, 1955, pp. 118–121.

18 For a discussion of the historical development of this legislation, see William D. Warren, "Regulation of Finance Charges in Retail Instalment Sales," *The Yale Law Journal,* April 1959, pp. 839–868.

by enabling legislation which provides higher ceilings. Commercial banks, consumer finance companies, credit unions, and industrial banks operate, in the main, under such laws. Commercial banks operate without instalment loan laws in seven states with usury ceilings where the legal status of charges above usury limits could be questioned.[19]

Three states (Arkansas, Oklahoma, and Tennessee) have constitutions which set interest ceilings at 10 per cent and which give no authority to legislatures to pass loan laws authorizing higher rates. Enabling cash loan legislation in these states must pass the test of constitutionality. Texas was in a similar situation until 1961 when it adopted a constitutional amendment permitting the legislature to pass loan laws with ceilings about 10 per cent.

---

[19] Arkansas, Louisiana, Montana, Nevada, Oklahoma, Tennessee, and Washington.

5. Consumer Knowledge of Finance Charges

THIS CHAPTER REVIEWS THE RESULTS of four surveys which were designed to test the extent of consumer awareness of finance charge information. Two of the surveys were in local areas with relatively small samples—Champaign and Urbana, Illinois (University of Illinois survey) and in the San Francisco Bay area (Lois Scott Hoskins' survey). The other two surveys were nationwide in scope and were made by the Survey Research Center of the University of Michigan and the National Bureau of Economic Research.

All four surveys investigated consumer knowledge of annual finance rates. Only the Illinois survey investigated consumer knowledge of dollar finance charges. The findings of all four surveys are similar and complementary, thus lending confidence to what is admittedly somewhat fragmentary evidence.

Illinois Survey

The Bureau of Economic and Business Research of the University of Illinois conducted a survey of a random sample of 311 families in Champaign and Urbana in the first quarter of 1954. One of the purposes of the survey was to ascertain the extent and accuracy of consumer knowledge of instalment charges. The following quotation gives the results: [1]

Although respondents readily answered questions relating to amounts of credit contracted, approximately two-thirds of the users of instalment credit did not know the amount of the carrying charge or interest rate on their most recent instalment purchase. An even smaller percentage of the families (24 per cent) who borrowed cash knew the carrying charges [dollar amounts] on the most recent loan, but almost one-half were aware of the interest rates paid on the most recent cash loan.

[1] Jean Mann Due, "Consumer Knowledge of Instalment Credit Charges," *The Journal of Marketing*, October 1955, p. 164. Only twenty families reported borrowing cash.

The study investigated the relation between the consumer's knowledge of charges and rates and his income, marital status, and occupation. "A higher percentage of families in the lower income classes knew the carrying charges than families in the upper income group. The opposite was true for knowledge of interest rates." No correlation was apparent between the number of years married and knowledge of carrying charges or interest rates, or between occupation and these factors.[2]

The study also examined the relation between knowledge of charges and rates and credit size, with the following results: [3]

One would expect, a priori, the existence of a direct correlation between the amount of credit extended and knowledge of charges and interest rates. A test of this hypothesis revealed that, contrary to expectations, a statistically significant inverse correlation (at the .05 probability level) existed between credit extended and knowledge of carrying charges. Forty-eight per cent of borrowers of amounts less than $200 knew the carrying charges, whereas 36 per cent of borrowers of $200 to $499 and only 18 per cent of those who borrowed more than $500 knew the charges on the most recent credit extended. There was, however, no significant difference in knowledge of interest rates by amounts of credit extended.

San Francisco Area Survey

In an interview study of 105 instalment buyers of new and used cars in the San Francisco Bay area, the interviewer asked each family what annual or simple (effective) interest rate it paid for instalment credit.[4] Seven respondents bought used cars from dealers who included the finance charge in the price of the car and said they paid no finance charge. Of the remaining ninety-eight respondents, 70 per cent said they did not know what rate they paid and 30 per

2 Ibid.

3 Ibid., pp. 164–165.

4 Lois Scott Hoskins, "Interest Rates Paid for Automobile Credit by San Francisco Bay Area Families," unpublished M.A. thesis, University of California, September 1958, p. 56. Mrs. Hoskins drew the names of 400 San Francisco Bay area car buyers at random from public registration records in Sacramento, California. One-half of the registrations were between November 17 and 23, 1956, and the other half between January 25 and 28, 1957. Mrs. Hoskins interviewed 105 of these families and the study results are based on these interviews. The other 295 families were eliminated for the following reasons: distance (57), business firms (15), impossibility to trace them (53), not at home (38), refusal to answer (16), employment of cars for business purposes (15), ineligibility for the study (100). The eligibility requirements were that (1) the family must include a husband and wife living together and (2) the credit must be obtained from some source other than a credit union.

cent gave answers which, with few exceptions, were considerably below the rates they actually paid (see Table 12). In three of the

TABLE 12

Distribution of Effective Annual Interest Rates Paid, According to Interest Rates Stated by Respondents, 1956–57

Rates Reported by Respondents (per cent)	Number of Respondents	Effective Annual Interest Rates Paid[a] (per cent)	
		Median	Range
3 or 4	3	11.6	7.7[b]–13.6
5 or 6	19	12.0	5.6[c]–20.3
7 or 8	6	20.8	11.5 –32.5
15	1	13.6	
Total	29	12.0	5.6[c]–32.5

SOURCE: Hoskins, "Interest Rates," p. 56.
a Computed by the constant ratio formula.
b Employee given a 4 per cent add-on rate by bank.
c Balloon contract for an automobile salesman.

four classes shown in the table the median rate actually paid is at least double the rates reported by respondents, and in two of the four classes the lowest rate paid is almost double the rates reported by respondents. In only one class is the reported rate approximately the same as the rate paid; this class includes one family. If reported rates were meant to signify add-on or discount rates, respondents may have estimated actual rates more closely than would appear. Yet if respondents believe that add-on or discount rates are the same as effective annual rates, the degree of underestimation remains the same.

Comparison of Tables 12 and 13 indicates that the rates actually paid by the twenty-nine respondents who stated what rate they paid (Table 13) fall in the same general range as the rates paid by all ninety-eight respondents.

Survey Research Center Survey

In a 1959 survey, the Survey Research Center of the University of Michigan asked consumers to state what finance charges they thought they would pay to finance a car on credit. Thirty-nine per cent gave too vague an answer to be coded or said they did not know. The remaining 61 per cent gave answers which covered a wide range. Since these answers were considered to be effective annual rates,[5] many consumers underestimated the finance rates they would pay. As indicated in Table 14, 37 per cent of those who gave usable answers said they would pay under 7 per cent in 1959, whereas only 5 per cent of new-car finance contracts were financed at effective rates of less than 7 per cent in 1954–55.[6]

TABLE 13

Distribution of Effective Annual Interest Rates Paid
by Respondents on New and Used Cars, 1956–57

Effective Annual Interest Rates[a] (per cent)	New Cars		Used Cars	
	Number	Per Cent	Number	Per Cent
4.9 – 5.9	3[b]	6.0	0	—
6.0 – 7.9	1	2.0	1	2.1
8.0 – 9.9	2	4.0	4	8.3
10.0 – 11.9	14	28.0	2	4.2
12.0 – 13.9	21	42.0	5	10.4
14.0 – 15.9	4	8.0	2	4.2
16.0 – 19.9	4	8.0	4	8.3
20.0 – 24.9	0	—	12	25.0
25.0 – 29.9	1	2.0	7	14.6
30.0 – 39.9	0	—	6	12.5
40.0 and over	0	—	5	10.4
Total	50	100.0	48	100.0

SOURCE: Hoskins, "Interest Rates," p. 31.
a Computed by the constant ratio formula.
b These contracts were one-year balloon contracts.

Because the question did not distinguish between new- and used-car financing, the degree of underestimation is even more marked than shown in Table 14, since used-car finance rates exceed new-car rates. On the other hand, it is possible that some consumers may have overestimated the rates they would have to pay. For 21 per cent said one would pay 16 per cent or more, whereas only 3 per

5 Interviewers converted some answers given in dollars to annual finance rates.
6 Available data indicate a slight rise in new-car finance rates from 1954–55 to 1959. The rise is not sufficient to change the results of comparing consumer answers in 1959 with new-car rates in 1954–55. For the trend of new-car finance rates, see Robert P. Shay, *New-Automobile Finance Rates, 1924–62*, NBER Occasional Paper 86, New York, 1963.

cent of the new-car contracts were actually financed in this range (Table 14). The data do not permit a realistic appraisal of the number of overestimates.

TABLE 14

Distribution of Consumer Estimates and Actual Finance
Rates on Auto Financing, 1954–55 and 1959
(per cent)

		Distribution of Actual Finance Rates[b]			
Annual Rate	Distribution of Consumer Estimates of Finance Rates, 1959[a]	All Credit Sources, 1954–55	Banks, 1954–55[c]	All Sales Finance Companies, 1954–55	Four Large Sales Finance Companies, 1959
Under 4	3	1	1	d	d
4 - 6.99	34	4	7	1	d
7 - 9.99	15	36	53	23	5
10 - 12.99	21	47	31	60	60
13 - 15.99	5	9	6	12	32
16 and over	21	3	3	3	2
	100	100	100	100	100

a Taken from November 1959 Interim Survey of the Survey Research Center of the University of Michigan. The question asked consumers is given in note a to Table 10. The percentages are based on usable responses. Nonusable responses (don't know, uncodable answers, or answers not ascertained) comprised 39 per cent of total responses.

b 1954–55 rates are based on data compiled by the Federal Reserve System. 1959 rates are compiled by the National Bureau. Effective rates are computed by the constant ratio formula.

c Includes direct and indirect financing.

d Less than .5 per cent.

NOTE: Detail may not add to total because of rounding.

It is possible that many consumers were thinking in terms of add-on or discount rates in giving the answers which underlie the computed figures in Table 14. In this event it is uncertain whether the implication of underestimation of the cost of credit is correct. However, if consumers actually believe that the concept of cost as measured by add-on or discount rates is equivalent to either simple or compound interest, there is a strong underestimate of credit cost when they make accurate statements of add-on or discount rates.

National Bureau-Consumers Union Survey

The National Bureau of Economic Research sent members of the

Consumers Union Members' Panel a questionnaire in the spring of 1960 which, among other things, asked for the information in Table 15.[7] There were 1,059 usable replies, of which 840 or 79 per cent reported rates (see last question of Table 15) and filled in sufficient other information to enable the National Bureau to determine annual finance rates; 219, or 21 per cent, of the replies did not report rates but did report sufficient other information to enable the National Bureau to compute annual finance rates. Table 16 gives, for four loan classes, the mean reported and mean computed finance rates for the 840 cases and the mean computed finance rates for the 219 cases.

TABLE 15

Question 25A, Reinterview Questionnaire, May 1960,
Consumers Union Members' Panel

Have you bought anything on the instalment plan since April 1958?

Yes ☐   No ☐

If yes, please write in the items in the boxes; then fill in the rest of the information as best you can remember. Otherwise skip to question 26.

Items Purchased on Instalment Plan

☐   ☐   ☐

Price of item   _____   _____   _____
Amount received on trade-in   _____   _____   _____
Cash down payment   _____   _____   _____
Amount borrowed   _____   _____   _____
Size of monthly payments   _____   _____   _____
Number of payments made   _____   _____   _____
Number of payments left   _____   _____   _____

Do your monthly payments include:
   Credit life insurance?   Yes ☐   No ☐
   Other insurance?   Yes ☐   No ☐
What interest rate did you have to pay?   ____%

Except for the $2,000-and-over loan-size class, mean reported rates tend to fall with size of loan. "Thus consumers seem to know that

[7] For a more detailed analysis of this survey, see F. Thomas Juster and Robert P. Shay, *Consumer Sensitivity to Finance Rates: An Empirical and Analytical Investigation,* NBER Occasional Paper 88, New York, 1964, Section II.

finance rates are appreciably higher on credit transactions involving relatively small (under $500) loan sizes than on credit transactions for larger loans." [8] They are not accurate, however, in reporting finance rates within each loan class. If both the type of commodity financed and the size of loan are held constant, there is no association between the rates actually paid and reported rates. In only one of twenty-four groups of credit transactions classified by type of commodity and loan size was there a statistically significant correlation (at the 5 per cent level) between actual rates and reported rates.[9]

Table 16 also indicates that the effective rates for nonreporting respondents are higher than for reporting respondents in each loan class. Since the differences ". . . are substantial only for the relatively few cases involving large loan sizes, failure to report rates does not, for the most part, seem to result in payment of appreciably higher rates. The evidence suggests that, for credit transactions involving relatively small loan sizes, households reporting rates are guessing, while those not reporting rates are admitting complete ignorance. In contrast, for credit transactions involving large loan sizes, the few nonreporting households paid appreciably more. We infer they had less information about rates and that lack of information was responsible for the high rates they paid." [10]

Juster and Shay present an alternative arrangement of the data to throw further light on the relation between rate knowledge and loan size. They divide respondents who reported rates into three groups: (1) those who reported rates roughly equal to the finance rate; (2) those who reported rates roughly equal to one-half the finance rate; and (3) all others. "The first group is an estimate of the maximum number of respondents who could be said to possess accurate information about effective annual rates; the second, an estimate of the maximum number to possess accurate information about add-on or discount rates; and the remainder, the minimum

---

8 *Ibid.*, p. 51. Consumers also seem to be aware that ". . . some classes of loans (automobile, home improvement) are likely to carry relatively low finance rates, others (furniture), to carry relatively high rates . . ." (*ibid.*, p. 59). Juster and Shay refer to this type of rate knowledge as "institutional knowledge."

9 *Ibid.*, p. 57.

10 *Ibid.*, p. 52.

TABLE 16

Distribution of Reported Annual Rates and Derived Finance Rates by Amount Borrowed

Amount Borrowed (dollars)	Respondents Reporting Rates				Respondents Not Reporting Rates			
	Number	Per Cent of Cases in Loan Class	Mean Rate f_r	Mean Rate f_a	Number	Per Cent of Cases in Loan Class	Mean Rate f_r	Mean Rate f_a
Under 500	440	71.7	9.4	30.8	174	28.3	—	32.2
500 - 999	113	82.5	7.4	19.5	24	17.5	—	20.8
1,000 - 1,999	207	92.4	6.9	13.8	17	7.6	—	18.6
2,000 and over	80	95.2	7.4	10.6	4	4.8	—	19.2
Total	840	79.3			219	20.7	—	
Mean			8.3	23.2				29.9

SOURCE: Juster and Shay, *Consumer Sensitivity*, p. 51.
NOTE f_r = reported annual finance rate; f_a = computed finance rate.

TABLE 17

Estimated Distribution and Mean Effective Rates of Sample of Households, Classified by Rate Information and Loan Size
(per cent)

Loan Size (dollars)	Sample Size	ESTIMATED DISTRIBUTION OF HOUSEHOLDS WITH[a]			Mean Effective Annual Finance Rates Paid			
		Accurate Information on		No Rate Infor- mation, Group 3	Group 1	Group 2	Group 3	Total
		Effective Rates, Group 1	Add-On Rates, Group 2					
Under 500	440	5.1	6.0	88.9	12.1	17.1	37.0	30.8
500 - 999	113	7.4	8.3	84.3	8.3	14.8	24.8	19.5
1,000 - 1,999	207	7.6	19.0	73.4	8.1	10.9	19.7	13.8
2,000 and over	80	10.6	20.3	69.1	7.2	11.0	13.7	10.6
Total	840	6.6	11.3	82.1				

SOURCE: Juster and Shay, *Consumer Sensitivity*, Table 8, p. 55.

[a] The procedure used in obtaining these percentages was as follows: (1) the proportions of cases in which the computed finance rate fell within plus or minus 2 percentage points of the reported rate were calculated (P_a); (2) the proportions of cases in which actual rates would have fallen within these ranges by chance were estimated (P_e); (3) P_e was subtracted from P_a; (4) the result was divided by the difference between 100 per cent and P_e (*ibid.*, p. 54, fn. 10).

number to possess neither kind of rate information." [11] The authors then estimate the probable proportions of each group of respondents with accurate rate information (see Table 17, note a) in order to analyze the results.

Table 17, which presents the results for these three groups by loan size, indicates that the extent of respondents' information about rates is inversely related to loan size. "Only 11 per cent of the respondents in the under $500 loan-size class appear to have any information about rates, and a majority of these knew only add-on or discount rates rather than effective annual finance rates. In contrast, about 30 per cent of the respondents in the over $2,000 loan class appear to have had fairly accurate rate information, predominantly about add-on or discount rates. In general, only a small proportion of the sample appears to have reasonably accurate information about rates charged on their own credit transactions." [12]

Table 18 is based on the same survey and provides support for the existence of a "6 per cent myth," i.e., the belief on the part of many credit users that they can obtain credit at an annual finance rate of 6 per cent. The table distributes the 840 respondents among twenty-one classes of computed annual finance rates, of which only one class includes 6 per cent. In sixteen of these twenty-one classes, 25 per cent or more of the respondents stated they were paying 6 per cent and in no class did the percentage fall below 12 per cent. The proportions of 6 per cent cases in each computed rate class show no upward or downward trend as the size of rate class increases. On the basis of other evidence collected by the Survey Research Center, George Katona states that ". . . many present-day users of instalment credit believe that the finance charges amount to 6 per cent or even less." [13]

Juster and Shay summarize the results of their study as follows: "First, few respondents had any awareness of the finance rates they had actually paid on instalment credit transactions. . . . If asked the price, they respond with essentially random figures. . . . Second,

11 *Ibid.*, p. 53.

12 *Ibid.*, pp. 54–55.

13 *Consumer Credit Labeling Bill,* Hearings before a Subcommittee of the Committee on Banking and Currency, U.S. Senate, 86th Congress, 2nd Session, Washington, 1960, p. 809.

despite the lack of rate knowledge, consumers appeared to know that certain kinds of credit cost more than others. . . . However, institutional knowledge, alone, cannot be expected to guarantee that borrowers will secure the lowest cost alternatives available to them. Third, the limited amount of rate information is mainly concentrated among unrationed consumers." [14]

TABLE 18

Respondents Reporting 6 Per Cent, by Class Intervals of Actual Rates Paid

Class Intervals of Actual Rates Paid (per cent)	Number of Respondents in Class (1)	Respondents Reporting 6 Per Cent	
		Number (2)	Per Cent (3)
Under 4.50	53	15	28
4.50 – 5.49	17	2	12
5.50 – 6.49	24	6	25
6.50 – 7.49	29	12	41
7.50 – 8.49	30	5	17
8.50 – 9.49	48	12	25
9.50 – 10.49	44	17	39
10.50 – 11.49	36	15	42
11.50 – 12.49	45	16	36
12.50 – 13.49	33	10	30
13.50 – 14.49	19	6	32
14.50 – 15.49	36	10	28
15.50 – 16.49	23	5	22
16.50 – 17.49	32	9	28
17.50 – 18.49	15	3	20
18.50 – 19.49	35	5	14
19.50 – 29.49	124	31	25
29.50 – 39.49	76	18	24
39.50 – 49.49	39	14	36
49.50 – 99.49	65	18	28
99.50 and over	17	5	29
Total	840	234	28

SOURCE: Juster and Shay, *Consumer Sensitivity*, pp. 60–61.

Concluding Remarks

The evidence from all four surveys suggests that relatively few

[14] Juster and Shay, *Consumer Sensitivity*, pp. 60, 73–74. To recall, they define "unrationed consumers" as consumers whose actual and preferred debt levels are the same; hence, their marginal borrowing cost is equal to (or less than) the going rates of primary lenders, i.e., banks and sales finance companies (*ibid.*, p. 14, 62–64).

consumers calculate finance rates with reasonable accuracy and that most consumers appear to believe that rate levels are substantially lower than they are in fact. The National Bureau survey also suggests that relatively few consumers calculate add-on or discount rates with reasonable accuracy. Neither the Michigan nor the NBER surveys ascertained whether respondents were reporting computational or effective rates. If consumers actually believe that the concept of cost as measured by add-on or discount rates is equivalent to either simple or compound interest, there is a strong underestimate of credit cost even when consumers know add-on or discount rates.

The National Bureau survey finding that consumers seem to know that relatively small loans cost more than relatively large loans and that auto credit is cheaper than most other forms of instalment credit implies some knowledge of rate differences among broad categories of credit transactions. In a similar vein is the Survey Research Center finding that the majority of consumers believe that banks are a lower-cost source of auto credit than car dealers.[15]

The Illinois survey also covered dollar charges and found that only a minority of consumers knew the amount of such charges on their most recent instalment purchase or instalment loan. None of the four surveys studied the extent of consumer knowledge of monthly rates or monthly payment size. While nothing can be said of monthly rate knowledge, there is strong empirical evidence elsewhere supporting the notion that consumers have reasonably accurate knowledge of monthly payment size because they have repeated payments to make. Arthur L. Broida, reporting on the pattern of response errors found in the 1954–55 Federal Reserve's New-Car Purchases Survey, stated that: "Nearly 80 per cent of the buyer reports on payments were within $1 of the lender reports, and the cases of difference were distributed very nearly symmetrically about zero in absolute terms."[16] Broida found that buyer recollections (from six to thirty months prior to the interview) of monthly pay-

15 George Katona, in *Consumer Credit Labeling Bill*, p. 807.
16 "Consumer Surveys as a source of Information for Social Accounting: The Problems," *The Flow-of-Funds Approach to Social Accounting*, Studies in Income and Wealth 26, Princeton for NBER, 1962, p. 375.

ments were markedly superior to their recollections of car price, total loan, or loan principal.

The findings of the four surveys are consistent with the widely held assumption that consumers have little knowledge of credit costs in terms of any of the varied forms of finance charge information. This conclusion is based upon answers to questions on either recent actual borrowings (the Illinois, San Francisco Area, and NBER-Consumers Union surveys) or a common hypothetical automobile-financing situation (the Survey Research Center survey).

Appendix A. Effects of Different Methods of Computing Finance Charges on Maturity Patterns of Finance Charges

FINANCING AGENCIES now use add-on, discount, and per cent per month methods to compute finance charges on individual instalment contracts. The first part of this appendix deals with the effects of each of these methods on the pattern of finance charges as maturities vary. In the second part, finance charges are assumed to be directly determined or computed in terms of effective rates, and the effects of different effective rate formulas on maturity patterns of finance charges are examined. This second situation exists in residential mortgage financing and is instructive for comparative purposes.

In both parts of the appendix we are interested in the maturity patterns of finance charges for varying periods of time rather than the absolute level of the finance charges at any one time. The latter is largely a function of the level of the rate used to compute the finance charge.

The analysis is carried on in both monthly and yearly time periods for several reasons. Some existing computational rates are monthly, some are yearly, most instalment contracts require monthly payments, and the year is a common period for financial analysis, financial reporting, and tax reporting.

Add-On, Discount, and Per Cent Per Month Rates

The maturity pattern of finance charges for each computational method is the same as the effective rate pattern for that method. Given this similarity, we can demonstrate the maturity pattern of finance charges for each method separately by determining, first, the equivalence of computational and effective rates under identical contract terms, and, second, the effect of different maturities on effective rates (the term structure). For any given computational rate, each of the several general computational methods results in a different effective rate level and an alternative term structure. The general order of these relationships differs for each computational method and is largely independent of computational rate levels.

TABLE A-1

Selected Computational Rates and Equivalent Effective
Monthly Finance Rates for Varying Maturities
(per cent)

Method of Computing Finance Charges	Computational Rate	Equivalent Effective Monthly Rates for Indicated Maturities in Months[a]					
		6	12	18	24	30	36
Annual add-on[b]	6	0.851	0.908	0.923	0.927	0.926	0.923
	8	1.133	1.205	1.221	1.223	1.219	1.212
	10	1.412	1.498	1.514	1.513	1.505	1.493
	12	1.691	1.788	1.804	1.798	1.785	1.767
	14	1.968	2.076	2.089	2.078	2.058	2.034
Annual discount[b]	6	.877	.965	1.012	1.049	1.082	1.115
	8	1.179	1.307	1.382	1.445	1.504	1.566
	10	1.486	1.659	1.770	1.867	1.966	2.071
	12	1.797	2.024	2.179	2.324	2.476	2.646
	14	2.113	2.400	2.609	2.813	3.040	3.302
Per cent per month[c]	1	1.000	1.000	1.000	1.000	1.000	1.000
	2	2.000	2.000	2.000	2.000	2.000	2.000
	3	3.000	3.000	3.000	3.000	3.000	3.000

[a] The equivalent effective monthly rates are based on a 360-day year and a 30-day month. There are in practice two ways of measuring a year, 360 or 365 days, and four ways of measuring a fractional part of a year. For a description of these four ways, see M. R. Neifeld, *Neifeld's Guide to Instalment Computations*, Easton, 1951, pp. 48–51.

[b] The equivalent effective monthly rates for the annual add-on and annual discount methods are based on the annuity principle, i.e., that each instalment payment is applied first to interest and any remaining amount is applied to reducing the principal.

[c] The effective monthly rates here apply to both per cent per month on declining balance and precomputation.

CHART A-1

Effective Monthly Finance Rates Equivalent
to Selected Annual Add-On, Annual Discount,
and Per Cent Per Month Rates on Monthly
Payment Contracts, by Maturity

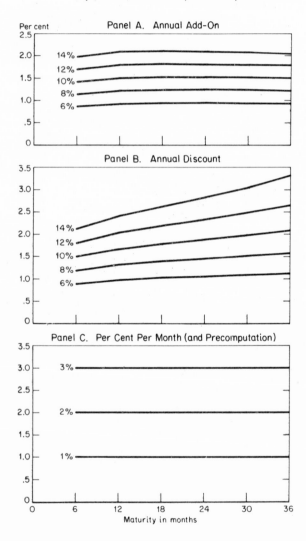

Source: Table A-1.

RELATIONSHIP OF ANNUAL ADD-ON, DISCOUNT, PER CENT PER MONTH, AND
PRECOMPUTATION TO EFFECTIVE MONTHLY AND ANNUAL FINANCE RATES

Table A-1 and Chart A-1 give for annual add-on, annual discount, per cent per month on declining balance, and precomputation the equivalence of selected computational rates and effective
monthly rates. They show that, as maturities lengthen, effective
monthly rates behave in the following way:

1. They stay the same under the per cent per month on declining
balance and precomputation methods.

2. They follow an inverted saucer pattern with the annual add-
on method. In general, the effective rate rises noticeably up to
twelve-month maturities and then rises more gradually for a time
thereafter as maturities lengthen. The maturity at which the effective monthly rate levels off becomes shorter as the add-on rate level
increases. The decline in effective rates starts after twenty-four
months with an 8 per cent annual add-on rate and after eighteen
months with a 14 per cent annual add-on rate. Monthly add-on
rates give an effective rate pattern similar to annual add-on rates,
except on revolving credit where they give a horizontal effective
rate pattern.

3. They rise quite markedly and continuously with discount.
Using a 6 per cent (annual) discount rate and a twelve-month contract for comparison, the effective monthly rate rises 8 per cent on
a twenty-four-month contract, 11 per cent on a thirty-month contract, and 16 per cent on a thirty-six-month contract. The corresponding percentages increase as maturities lengthen and become
successively higher with higher discount rates.

A number of state laws providing ceiling rates on cash lending
and retail instalment financing contain maturity limits. In such
laws which designate discount or discount plus, the usual maturity
limits range from twenty-five to sixty-one months. Thus a single
discount computational rate ceiling results in progressively higher
effective rate ceilings up to the maturity limit.

Assuming no change in maturity patterns during a year and no
change in the amount of loanable funds, a financing agency's total
annual finance charges are twelve times its monthly finance charges.
While there is no conflict about the relation between annual and

monthly finance charges, there are two conflicting views on how to establish the equivalent level of effective rates for a given computational rate. This conflict concerns level rather than pattern. Both views give effective annual rates which vary with maturity in patterns similar to those shown in Table A-1 for effective monthly rates. While we cannot end the conflict about level, we can indicate the assumption underlying each view.

According to one view, effective annual rates are twelve times the corresponding effective monthly rates. For convenience, we call these annually based effective annual rates, or y_a for short.[1] According to the second view, effective annual finance rates are obtained by compounding effective monthly rates according to the following formula:

$$y_m = (1 + k)^{12},$$

where y_m is the effective annual rate and k is the effective monthly rate, as shown in Table A-1.[2] For convenience, we call these monthly based effective annual rates, or y_m for short.

Table A-2 gives y_a and y_m for several selected computational rates. The y_a rates are based on the assumption that a year is the time limit for compounding (i.e., the compounding interval) and the y_m rates are based on a compounding interval of one month. They are two methods of measuring effective annual finance rates, much as yards and meters are two methods of measuring length.

To illustrate, the effective monthly rate for a twelve-month contract at a 6 per cent add-on rate is .9083 per cent (rounded off to .908 per cent in Table A-1). If a year is used as the compounding interval, the equivalent effective annual rate is $12 \times .9083$ per cent, or 10.90 per cent.

If a month is used as the compounding interval, the effective annual rate is equal to $(1 + .9083\%)^{12} - 1$, or 11.46 per cent, i.e., the effective monthly rate times a compound interest factor. The reasoning here is that, since a month is the compounding interval, pay-

---

[1] See Ralph A. Young and associates, *Personal Finance Companies and Their Credit Practices*, New York, NBER, 1940, p. 127, and M. R. Neifeld, "Analysis of Methods of Computing Interest on Amortized Loans," *Bankers Monthly*, March 1938, p. 135.

[2] See Milan V. Ayres, *Instalment Mathematics Handbook*, New York, 1946, pp. 233–235.

ment of 91 cents a month for twelve months represents a higher yearly rate than payment of twelve times 91 cents or $10.92 in one payment at the end of the year. This is based on the assumption that the debtor, in paying 91 cents a month, is deprived of earning the interest that he could have earned on that money if he had invested the 91 cents at interest each month and made one payment at the end of the year.

TABLE A-2

Selected Computational Rates and Equivalent Effective
Annual Finance Rates for Varying Maturities
(per cent)

Method of Computing Finance Charges	Computa-tional Rate	Symbol[a]	Equivalent Effective Annual Rates for Indicated Maturities in Months[b]					
			6	12	18	24	30	36
Annual add-on	6	y_a	10.21	10.90	11.08	11.12	11.11	11.08
	6	y_m	10.72	11.46	11.67	11.72	11.71	11.66
Discount	6	y_a	10.52	11.58	12.14	12.59	12.98	13.38
	6	y_m	11.06	12.15	12.80	13.37	13.74	14.23
Per cent per month[c]	3	y_a	36.00	36.00	36.00	36.00	36.00	36.00
	3	y_m	42.58	42.58	42.58	42.58	42.58	42.58

[a] The symbol y_a means yearly based effective annual rates. These rates are twelve times corresponding monthly effective rates. The figures shown were obtained by using effective monthly rates to four decimal places and thus vary slightly from twelve times the two-decimal rates shown in Table A-1.

The symbol y_m means monthly based effective annual rates. These rates were determined by the formula $y = (1 + k)^{12} - 1$, where y_m is the effective annual rate and k is the effective monthly rate. To illustrate, the monthly based effective annual rate on a twelve-month instalment contract at an annual add-on rate of 6 per cent is: $(1 + .9083\%)^{12} - 1 = 11.46\%$. The .9083% is shown rounded off to .91% in Table A-1.

[b] The effective annual rates are based on a 360-day year and a 30-day month.

[c] The effective annual rates here apply to both per cent per month on declining balance and precomputation.

The conflict is essentially over the compounding interval.[3] It does not directly concern financing agencies and sellers under present conditions because their monthly and yearly finance charges are not

[3] See Le Baron R. Foster, "Instalment Credit Costs and the Consumer," *Journal of Business*, January 1935, pp. 31–34. There are, of course, other possible compounding intervals besides a year and a month, e.g., a quarter, a half-year, a week, a day, and infinitely small intervals of time.

affected by which yardstick is used and they are not required to quote effective annual rates to consumers.

RELATIONSHIP OF ANNUAL ADD-ON PLUS AND DISCOUNT PLUS TO
EFFECTIVE MONTHLY AND ANNUAL FINANCE RATES

The main question here is the effect of maturity on effective rate patterns when a service or investigation charge is added to an annual add-on or discount charge in determining the finance charge. The usual form of additional charge is a flat per cent of principal owed or borrowed, ranging from 1 to 8 per cent, with 1 to 4 per cent being most common. In some laws, the additional charge is subject to a maximum dollar limit, usually from $10 to $25. Table A-3 shows that lengthening maturities cause effective monthly rates to fall with annual add-on plus and to rise, fall, or behave in a U-shaped manner with annual discount plus. These patterns are not altered if the additional charge is subject to a flat dollar limit. The effect of such a limit is to lower effective monthly rates as loan size increases but to leave unchanged the maturity pattern of effective monthly rates for any given loan size. The loan-size effect is not a function of the method of computing finance charges but of the rate levels.

The patterns in Table A-3 result from the fact that the additional charge is a flat amount and does not, like the add-on or discount charge, increase proportionately as maturity lengthens in periodic intervals. This causes the "over-all annual charge" rate to fall as maturity lengthens. Thus, with an annual add-on rate of 6 per cent and an additional charge of 2 per cent, the over-all annual charge rate is 8 per cent on a twelve-month contract and 7 per cent on a twenty-four-month contract. The downward pull of the additional charge as maturity lengthens (1) meets the inverted saucer effect on annual add-on as shown in Table A-1 and causes the annual add-on-plus pattern to fall, and (2) meets the rising effect of annual discount as shown in Table A-1 and causes the varying discount-plus patterns shown in Table A-3; each pattern depends on the relative strength of the downward and upward pulls.

In a few discount-plus laws, the additional charge is determined on a sliding scale, e.g., 8 per cent on the first $600 of principal owed and 4 per cent on any excess. This arrangement does not alter the maturity patterns shown in Table A-3. It is simply another way of varying over-all annual charge rates by loan size rather than by maturity for any given loan size. In at least one law, the additional charge is computed as a function of the principal owed and time. The maturity patterns in this case are the same as those in Table A-1.

Effective Rates

The discussion in the first part of this appendix has been based on the assumption that finance charges are computed by using add-on, discount, and per cent per month rates and that effective rates are derived from finance charges so computed. We call this situation 1. This second part is based on the assumption that finance charges and finance charge ceilings are determined directly from effective rates. We call this situation 2.

TABLE A-3

Equivalent Effective Monthly Rates for Selected Annual Add-On Plus and Annual Discount-Plus Computational Rates for Varying Maturities
(per cent)

Annual Add-On or Discount Rate[a]	Additional Charge in Per Cent of Principal Owed	Effective Monthly Rates for Indicated Maturities in Months		
		12	24	36
6	1	1.06	1.00	.97
6	2	1.21	1.08	1.04
6	4	1.50	1.22	1.12
6	1	1.13	1.14	1.20
6	2	1.31	1.24	1.26
6	4	1.49	1.45	1.42
10	1	1.84	1.98	2.17
10	2	2.02	2.09	2.25
10	4	2.40	2.32	2.45

[a] The first three are add-on rates; the others are discount rates.

As has already been shown, in situation 1 the choice of the formula used to determine effective rates does not have any influence on the gross revenue of financing agencies. In situation 2 the choice of the formula affects the gross revenue of financing agencies, for different formulas give different maturity patterns of finance charges.[4]

To illustrate situation 2, assume a $1,000 contract on which dollar finance charges are based on an effective annual rate of 12 per cent. The dollar finance charges for varying maturities under each of several formulas are as follows:

	Finance Charge in Dollars		
Formula	12-Month Contract	24-Month Contract	36-Month Contract
Monthly based annuity formula (y_m)[5]	62.67	122.76	185.03
Constant ratio formula (y_c)	65.00	125.00	185.00
Annually based annuity formula (y_a)[6]	66.19	129.76	195.72

The differences in dollar charges are as follows:

	Differences in Finance Charges in Dollars		
Item	12-Month Contract	24-Month Contract	36-Month Contract
Excess of y_c over y_m	2.33	2.24	− .03
Excess of y_a over y_c	1.19	4.76	10.72

As the above example shows, the y_m formula gives somewhat lower finance charges than the y_c formula on shorter maturities, with the differences narrowing progressively as maturities lengthen. Compared with the y_c formula, the y_a (or y_d) formula gives slightly higher finance charges on shorter maturities and progressively higher dollar charges as maturities lengthen. The y_m charges are lower than the y_c charges because, as Chart 1 shows, the compounding effect is stronger with the y_m formula and hence a lower dollar charge is needed to get a given effective rate (12 per cent in our sample). The difference in compounding effect also explains why the y_c dollar charge is higher than the y_a (or y_d) dollar charge.

If a state were to adopt any one formula in setting effective rate

4 See Robert W. Johnson, *Methods of Stating Finance Charges*, Columbia University, New York, 1961, pp. 113–118.

5 This formula is based on monthly compounding.

6 This formula is based on yearly compounding. The y_d formula gives roughly the same figures as the y_a formula and is not shown separately.

ceilings, the formula adopted would, relative to other possible formulas, introduce a different maturity pattern of charges. This problem is not unique to situation 2, however, for, as has been shown
earlier in this appendix, the same problem arises in situation 1,
i.e., the add-on, discount, and per cent per moth methods of computing finance charges contain differences in maturity patterns of
finance charges. The maturity pattern problem is thus independent
of the existence of effective rates or, given their existence, of
whether they are derivative or computational rates.

Appendix B. Equivalent Effective Monthly and Annual Finance Rates Converted from Annual Add-On and Discount Rates for Selected Even Monthly Payment Contract Maturities

TABLE B-1

Equivalent Effective Annual Finance Rates for Selected Annual Add-On Rates with Varying Contract Maturities and Even Monthly Payments

(per cent)

Annual Add-On Rate	Annuity Method with Interest Compounded Annually (maturity in months)						Annuity Method with Interest Compounded Monthly (maturity in months)					
	6	12	18	24	30	36	6	12	18	24	30	36
4	6.82	7.30	7.44	7.49	7.51	7.51	7.05	7.55	7.68	7.76	7.78	7.78
4 1/2	7.67	8.20	8.36	8.41	8.42	8.41	7.94	8.52	8.69	8.74	8.76	8.74
5	8.52	9.10	9.27	9.32	9.33	9.31	8.86	9.50	9.67	9.73	9.73	9.67
6	10.21	10.90	11.08	11.12	11.11	11.08	10.72	11.46	11.67	11.72	11.71	11.66
7	11.89	12.67	12.86	12.91	12.89	12.84	12.55	13.45	13.68	13.71	13.69	13.62
8	13.60	14.46	14.65	14.68	14.63	14.54	14.44	15.45	15.68	15.71	15.67	15.52
9	15.28	16.24	16.42	16.43	16.36	16.25	16.39	17.49	17.72	17.73	17.61	17.45
10	16.94	17.98	18.17	18.16	18.06	17.92	18.20	19.53	19.77	19.75	19.64	19.45
11	18.62	19.72	19.91	19.87	19.74	19.57	20.27	21.54	21.84	21.77	21.62	21.41
12	20.29	21.46	21.65	21.58	21.42	21.20	22.29	23.70	24.03	23.84	23.65	23.39
13	21.94	23.17	23.36	23.26	23.05	22.80	24.33	25.78	26.09	25.89	25.64	25.33
14	23.62	24.91	25.07	24.94	24.70	24.41	26.37	27.95	28.30	28.02	27.74	27.35
15	25.27	26.63	26.76	26.58	26.29	25.98	28.41	30.16	30.31	30.07	29.73	29.33
17	28.57	30.02	30.11	29.84	29.47	29.06	32.63	34.48	34.62	34.33	33.77	33.22

(continued)

TABLE B-1 (concluded)

Annual Add-On Rate	Constant Ratio Method (maturity in months)						Effective Monthly Rates, Both Annuity Methods (maturity in months)					
	6	12	18	24	30	36	6	12	18	24	30	36
4	6.86	7.39	7.58	7.68	7.74	7.78	.57	.61	.61	.62	.63	.63
4 1/2	7.71	8.32	8.53	8.64	8.71	8.76	.64	.68	.70	.70	.70	.70
5	8.57	9.24	9.47	9.60	9.68	9.73	.71	.76	.77	.78	.78	.78
6	10.28	11.09	11.37	11.52	11.61	11.68	.85	.91	.92	.93	.93	.92
7	12.00	12.94	13.26	13.44	13.55	13.62	.99	1.06	1.07	1.08	1.07	1.07
8	13.71	14.79	15.16	15.36	15.48	15.57	1.13	1.21	1.22	1.22	1.22	1.21
9	15.43	16.64	17.05	17.28	17.42	17.51	1.27	1.35	1.37	1.37	1.36	1.35
10	17.14	18.49	18.95	19.20	19.35	19.46	1.41	1.50	1.51	1.51	1.51	1.49
11	18.86	20.34	20.84	21.12	21.29	21.41	1.55	1.64	1.66	1.66	1.65	1.63
12	20.57	22.19	22.74	23.04	23.26	23.35	1.69	1.79	1.80	1.80	1.79	1.77
13	22.28	24.04	24.63	24.96	25.16	25.30	1.83	1.93	1.95	1.94	1.92	1.90
14	24.00	25.89	26.53	26.88	27.10	27.24	1.97	2.08	2.09	2.08	2.06	2.03
15	25.71	27.73	28.42	28.80	29.03	29.19	2.11	2.22	2.23	2.22	2.19	2.17
17	29.14	31.43	32.21	32.64	32.90	33.08	2.38	2.50	2.51	2.49	2.46	2.42

TABLE B-2

Equivalent Effective Annual Finance Rates for Selected Annual
Discount Rates with Varying Contract Maturities and
Even Monthly Payments

(per cent)

Annual Discount Rate	Annuity Method with Interest Compounded Annually (maturity in months)						Annuity Method with Interest Compounded Monthly (maturity in months)					
	6	12	18	24	30	36	6	12	18	24	30	36
4	6.99	7.60	7.91	8.13	8.32	8.49	7.21	7.87	8.20	8.45	8.64	8.83
4 1/2	7.85	8.58	8.95	9.22	9.45	9.66	8.14	8.84	9.33	9.61	9.86	9.98
5	8.74	9.57	10.00	10.32	10.60	10.87	9.09	9.77	10.47	10.82	11.11	11.43
6	10.52	11.58	12.14	12.59	12.98	13.38	11.06	12.15	12.84	13.34	13.74	14.23
7	12.32	13.61	14.34	14.93	15.47	16.02	12.82	14.43	15.32	15.99	16.64	17.25
8	14.15	15.68	16.58	17.34	18.05	18.79	14.84	16.90	17.87	18.72	19.58	20.54
9	15.97	17.78	18.88	19.84	20.77	21.73	17.19	19.28	20.57	21.71	22.86	24.02
10	17.83	19.91	21.24	22.40	23.59	24.85	19.31	21.84	23.43	24.88	26.20	27.88
11	19.69	22.09	23.66	25.10	26.58	28.20	21.54	24.46	26.37	28.20	30.12	32.15
12	21.56	24.29	26.15	27.89	29.71	31.75	23.88	27.14	29.51	31.72	34.14	36.87
13	23.46	26.53	28.68	30.76	33.00	35.53	26.16	29.98	32.78	35.44	38.47	41.91
14	25.36	28.80	31.31	33.76	36.48	39.62	28.48	32.92	36.23	39.43	43.26	48.16
15	27.29	31.13	34.00	36.90	40.16	44.05	30.92	35.93	39.78	43.83	48.50	54.10
17	31.20	35.88	39.62	43.57	48.24	54.13	37.03	42.43	47.64	53.42	60.44	69.79

(continued)

TABLE B-2 (concluded)

Annual Discount Rate	Constant Ratio Method (maturity in months)						Effective Monthly Rates, Both Annuity Methods (maturity in months)					
	6	12	18	24	30	36	6	12	18	24	30	36
4	7.00	7.69	8.06	8.34	8.60	8.84	.58	.63	.66	.68	.69	.71
4 1/2	7.89	8.70	9.14	9.49	9.81	10.12	.65	.72	.74	.77	.79	.81
5	8.79	9.72	10.24	10.67	10.94	11.45	.73	.80	.83	.86	.87	.91
6	10.60	11.78	12.49	13.09	13.66	14.24	.88	.97	1.01	1.05	1.08	1.12
7	12.43	13.90	14.82	15.63	16.42	17.24	1.03	1.13	1.20	1.24	1.29	1.34
8	14.29	16.05	17.22	18.29	19.35	20.48	1.18	1.31	1.38	1.45	1.50	1.57
9	16.16	18.26	19.71	21.07	22.48	23.99	1.33	1.48	1.57	1.65	1.73	1.81
10	18.05	20.51	22.29	24.00	25.81	27.80	1.49	1.66	1.77	1.87	1.97	2.07
11	19.95	22.82	24.96	27.08	29.37	31.95	1.64	1.84	1.97	2.09	2.22	2.35
12	21.88	25.17	27.73	30.32	33.18	36.49	1.80	2.02	2.18	2.32	2.48	2.65
13	23.83	27.59	30.60	33.73	37.28	41.47	1.96	2.21	2.39	2.56	2.75	2.96
14	25.81	30.05	33.58	37.33	41.69	46.97	2.11	2.40	2.61	2.81	3.04	3.30
15	27.80	32.58	36.67	41.14	46.45	53.07	2.27	2.59	2.83	3.08	3.35	3.67
17	31.85	37.36	43.24	49.45	57.22	67.51	2.60	2.99	3.30	3.63	4.02	4.51

Appendix C. State Supervisors' Opinions on the Ability of Financing Agencies to Convert Finance Charges to Effective Annual Rates

Table C-1 gives the opinions of state supervisors of Consumer Credit agencies on the ability of the personnel of financing agencies to compute effective rates with and without the aid of rate tables. Of the twenty-five who answered the question assuming no use of rate tables, twenty-two felt that relatively few financing agencies could determine effective rates. Of the forty who answered the question asuming the use of rate tables, twenty-four felt that the personnel in all financing agencies could determine effective rates, fourteen felt that most financing agencies could do so, and two felt that relatively few could do so.

The data in Table C-1 are admittedly fragmentary and do not provide conclusive evidence of the extent to which employees of financing agencies have the ability to compute effective rates with and without the aid of finance rate tables. Also the data do not cover employees of sellers.

Table C-1 suggests two points, however. One is the possibility that some financing agencies and—by extension—some sellers may not be able to determine effective rates. The other is the sharp contrast in the pattern of distribution of supervisor opinion of the ability of the agencies to determine effective rates with and without the aid of rate tables.

The stress supervisors put on the usefulness of rate tables or charts has a parallel in present practice. Financing agencies and sellers now rely heavily on rate charts to determine dollar finance charges in the manner required by existing laws. These charts usually include one or more computational rates and give the dollar finance charges for varying maturities and loan sizes for each computational rate desired. Effective monthly or annual rates could be worked out and included in these charts. A chart covering one or several computational rates, e.g., an add-on rate of 7 per cent, could show the dollar finance charge and the effective monthly or annual rate for each computational rate for different maturity and loan size.[1] For example, on a rate chart for a computational annual add-on rate of 7 per cent which is based on the constant ratio formula for determining effective rates, the effective annual rate would be shown as 13.26

TABLE C-1

State Supervisor Opinions on the Ability of the Personnel of
Financing Agencies to Determine Finance Rates

Financing Agencies	Able to Determine Rates Without the Aid of Finance Rate Tables		Able to Determine Rates With the Aid of Finance Rate Tables	
	Number	Per Cent	Number	Per Cent
All	0	0	24	60
Most	3	12	14	35
Relatively few	22	88	2	5
Total	25[b]	100	40[b]	100

SOURCE: The question asked was: "Do you think financing agencies have personnel with sufficient knowledge to be able to determine accurately a monthly or yearly financing rate on any instalment credit transaction?"

	Without the Aid of Prepared Effective Financing Rate Tables*	With the Aid of Prepared Effective Financing Rate Tables*
a. All financing agencies?	Yes——— No———	Yes——— No———
b. Most financing agencies?	Yes——— No———	Yes——— No———
c. Relatively few financing agencies?	Yes——— No———	Yes——— No———

*Effective financing rate tables are similar to bond yield tables.
a The difference between each total and 43 represents the number of supervisors who either failed to answer the question or gave an uncodable answer.

1 For examples of tables containing effective rates, see *Financial Compound Interest and Annuity Tables,* Boston, 1947, and *Table for Converting Interest Rates into Discount Charges and Discount Charges into Interest Rates,* Chicago, 1958.

per cent for eighteen-month instalment credit transactions of all sizes. For other examples, see Tables B-1 and B-2.

It should be emphasized that any effective rates on rate charts are *ex ante* rates. Sellers and financing agencies cannot determine *ex post* effective rates when they extend credit for they cannot know to what extent, if any, borrowers will deviate from planned payment schedules during the life of the contract.

The cost of rate charts depends on a number of factors, including the number of computational rates included and quantity ordered. To give some idea of the cost of existing computational rate charts, one company currently (1964) quotes prices ranging downward from 20 cents a chart on purchases of twenty-five copies to $3\frac{1}{2}$ cents a chart on purchases of 2,000. Each chart shows the dollar finance charge computed at the specified computational rate for varying loan sizes and maturities.

Appendix D. Prepayment, Refinancing, Extension, and Delinquency

Many, if not most, consumer financing laws contain provisions governing the adjustments of charges on instalment contracts which are paid ahead of or behind schedule. The general nature of these provisions and the issues they raise are described in the first part of this appendix and the relation of these provisions to rate computation and quotation is discussed in the second part.

Contracts are paid ahead of schedule either through prepayment or refinancing. Prepayment may be full or partial. Prepayment in full is complete cash payment of an instalment contract before maturity. Partial prepayment is cash payment of one or several instalments before they are due. Refinancing is full payment of an instalment contract before maturity coincident with the signing of a new instalment contract with the same creditor, often in connection with a new instalment purchase.

Contracts which are not paid on schedule are technically in default or delinquency. In such cases and in cases in which the borrower anticipates that he may not be able to meet a scheduled payment, the borrower and lender may agree to extend the contract. Extension (deferment, renewal) consists in moving one or more instalment payments of an existing contract to a later point in time.

Available data on refinancing, extension, and delinquency indicate they are common practices. There is no available evidence on the extent of prepayment in full and prepayment in part.

Frequency of Refinancing and Extension. The data presented in Chapter 2 covering several states show that a high proportion (from 65 to 80 per cent) of consumer finance company loans are refinanced or extended.[1] Data covering New York commercial banks for 1939 to 1944 indicate that renewal and refinanced personal loans varied from 23 to 30 per cent of total personal loans made in those years.[2] The corresponding figure is 27 per cent in a 1950–51 study covering banks in a number of states.[3] A 1941 study of New York industrial banks indicates that 34 per cent of their loans were renewed or refinanced.[4]

In the Federal Reserve survey of 1954–55 new-car buyers, 8 per cent of the 1954 instalment buyers and 4 per cent of the 1955 instalment buyers had "refinanced" their car debts by the middle of 1956.[5] As defined in the study, refinancing does not include the elimination of existing debt through trade-ins. When buyers traded in their cars, any outstanding debt was considered to have been paid off rather than refinanced. This is a narrower definition of refinancing than the usual one [6] and helps account for the much lower refinancing percentages in the Federal Reserve study than in the instalment cash lending studies cited in the above paragraphs.

The following evidence suggests that refinancing through trading in an existing car for a new car is not uncommon. First, of the new-car buyers in 1954 about 5 per cent had bought a new car within the preceding twelve months and about 17 per cent within the preceding twelve to twenty-three months. Corresponding percentages for the 1955 new-car buyers were 7 and around 20.[7] Some of these buyers probably refinanced, for approximately two-thirds of new cars are bought on credit and over 86 per cent of the 1954–55 new-car financing contracts had maturities longer than twenty-four months and over 53 per cent had maturities of thirty months or more.

1 For a detailed breakdown by type of company, see John M. Chapman and Frederick W. Jones, *An Analysis of the Current Financial Status of Licensed Lenders in the State of New York*, Columbia University, New York, 1958, p. 55.

2 "Analysis of Operations of Personal Loan Departments of Banks and Trust Companies, 1939–1944," New York State Banking Department, 1945, p. 8.

3 W. David Robbins, *Consumer Instalment Loans*, Columbus, 1955, p. 82.

4 *Special Report on Licensed Lenders*, New York State Banking Department, Albany, 1946, p. 9.

5 *Consumer Instalment Credit, Part IV, Financing New Car Purchases*, Federal Reserve System, Washington, 1957, pp. 82–83.

6 See *ibid.*, p. 143.

7 *Ibid.*, p. 21.

Maturities were probably somewhat, though not appreciably, shorter in the years immediately before 1954.

Second, as of the middle of 1956, 11 per cent of those who bought new cars in 1954 and 1955 had already disposed of these cars, mostly while buying a new car.[8] In view of the high percentage of credit buyers and the prevalence of financing contracts of longer than twenty-four months, some of these buyers probably refinanced existing instalment contracts when they bought their new cars.

Third, 39 per cent of the 1954–55 new-car buyers still had debt on their 1954–55 purchases in the middle of 1956. Of this group, 11 per cent expected to buy a new car within twelve months, 26 per cent expected to buy a new car within thirteen to thirty months, and 26 per cent were uncertain.[9] Because over 53 per cent of the 1954–55 new-car finance contracts had maturities of thirty months or more, some of this group probably refinanced existing instalment contracts when they bought their new cars. Thus, we conclude that refinancing and extension are common practices in new-car financing, as well as in most segments of cash lending.

Frequency of Delinquency or Default. Over the postwar period until 1962, monthly delinquency rates among six types of bank instalment financing ranged from under .5 to over 3 per cent.[10] (The corresponding range of unweighted average delinquency rates of all six types of financing combined was roughly between .8 and 2.1 per cent.)

These data plus data on delinquency and repossession rates for various financing agencies for varying years from 1925 to 1956 suggest that all financing agencies have some delinquencies at any given time and that delinquencies vary through time for each

---

[8] *Ibid.,* p. 102.

[9] *Ibid.*

[10] *Delinquency Rates on Bank Instalment Loans,* a monthly report of the Instalment Credit Commission, American Bankers Association. The six types of instalment financing are auto direct, auto indirect, FHA Title I, home appliance, conventional property improvement, and personal. Delinquency rates for each type of financing are determined as follows: (1) for each bank, the percentage that the number of instalment contracts with an instalment past due for thirty days or more is of the total number of accounts outstanding on the same date; and (2) for the sample of banks as a whole, an unweighted average of the delinquency rates of the reporting banks.

agency.[11] The factors that influence the level of an agency's delinquency rate(s) at any time and changes in its delinquency rate(s)
through time include the types of instalment financing in which it
engages, income and other characteristics of its borrowers, its lending terms and standards, the extent of its efforts to reduce delinquencies, the general level and direction of employment and
income, and area economic conditions including duration of de-
pressed conditions in a distress area.[12] Our discussion indicates that
delinquency is an ever-present problem for financing agencies.

Legislative Provisions

In describing legislative provisions on prepayment, refinancing,
extension, and delinquency, it is necessary to distinguish between
advance-charge and post-charge laws. An advance-charge law is one
which specifies a computational method under which finance
charges are computed in advance, e.g., add-on, add-on plus, discount,
discount plus, or precomputation. A post-charge law is one which
specifies a computational method under which the finance charge
is computed at the end of each payment period, i.e., per cent per
month. The importance of the distinction will become clear from
the discussion here.

ADVANCE-CHARGE LAWS

Provisions governing prepayment, refinancing, extension, and delinquency are common in advance-charge laws. They are found in
most retail instalment financing laws, most of the small-loan laws
which permit precomputation or annual add-on, and a growing
number of instalment and industrial loan laws.

Prepayment in Full and Refinancing. Instalment credit users can
prepay instalment contracts in full at any time. They are not legally entitled to any refund of prepaid finance charges, however,
unless such refunds are specified in their contracts or are required

11 For a detailed analysis of available delinquency and repossession data from
1925 to 1956, see Geoffrey H. Moore, Thomas R. Atkinson, and Philip A. Klein,
"Changes in the Quality of Consumer Instalment Credit," *Consumer Instalment
Credit,* Board of Governors of the Federal Reserve Sytsem, Washington, 1957,
Part II, Vol. I, pp. 79–113.
12 *Ibid.*

by law. Prepayment in full is at the borrower's initiative. Refinancing may be at the borrower's or creditor's initiative. Financing agencies and sellers often encourage refinancing in order to sell more credit or more goods.

The principle is now firmly established in legislation that financing agencies and sellers should refund some portion of finance charges paid in advance on instalment contracts which are paid in full or refinanced before maturity. Prepayment refunds are required in virtually all retail instalment financing laws, virtually all small-loan laws which permit advance charges, over half of the instalment loan laws, and over half of the industrial loan laws. Of the forty-three supervisors in the State Supervisor Survey, forty-two favored prepayment refunds and one expressed no opinion.

Determination of the Amount of Prepayment Refunds.—Most of the laws which require prepayment refunds specify that refunds are to be computed by the direct ratio formula, also known as the "sum of the digits" or "rule of 78" method. A few laws specify the annuity method, also called the pro-rata method, and a few do not specify any method. The "rule of 78" method is favored by most of the supervisors in the State Supervisor Survey and has wide industry acceptance. Of the forty-three supervisors in the survey, thirty-nine favored the "rule of 78" method, one favored the pro-rata method, one favored both, and two expressed no opinion.

The direct ratio or "rule of 78" method of computing refunds is usually stated in the following legal language: The purchaser shall receive a refund of charges which shall be at least as great a proportion of the total charges as the sum of the remaining monthly balance of the principal and interest combined scheduled to follow the date of prepayment is of the sum of all the monthly balances of principal and interest combined originally scheduled by the contract. The method may be illustrated as follows: Assume a twelve-month instalment contract in which the amount to be financed is $2,400 and the finance charge is equal to an annual add-on rate of 8 per cent or $192. The borrower's monthly payment is $216 ($2,592 ÷ 12). Under the direct ratio method, the finance charge is assumed to be earned each month as follows:

Month	Balance of Principal Owed (dollars)	Ratio of Balance of Principal Owed to Cumulative Principal [13]	Fraction of Finance Charge Earned [14]	Ratio of Principal Owed and Finance Charge Earned to Total Principal and Total Finance Charge	Finance Charge Earned (dollars)
1	2,400	12/78	12/78	12/78	29.54
2	2,200	11/78	11/78	11/78	27.08
3	2,000	10/78	10/78	10/78	24.62
4	1,800	9/78	9/78	9/78	22.15
5	1,600	8/78	8/78	8/78	19.69
6	1,400	7/78	7/78	7/78	17.23
7	1,200	6/78	6/78	6/78	14.77
8	1,000	5/78	5/78	5/78	12.31
9	800	4/78	4/78	4/78	9.85
10	600	3/78	3/78	3/78	7.38
11	400	2/78	2/78	2/78	4.92
12	200	1/78	1/78	1/78	2.46
78	15,600				192.00

Suppose the instalment borrower pays the contract in full right after the fifth payment. Including the fifth payment, he has paid $1,080. If no prepayment refund is made, he owes $1,512 ($2,592–$1,080). If a prepayment refund is made by the direct ratio method, the borrower is entitled to a refund of 28/78 of the finance charge, or $68.92, and must make a final payment of $1,443.08 ($2,592–$1,080–$68.92). The fraction 28/78 is the sum of the fractions from the sixth through the twelfth months.[15]

Offsets Against Prepayment Refunds.—Some state financing laws provide offsets against prepayment refunds. Provisions for determining these offsets often vary among laws in the same state; this

[13] The cumulative principal is $15,600 in this example.

[14] The numerators of the fraction are the numbers of the months in the contract in reverse chronological order. The denominator is the sum of the months in the contract, i.e., numbers 1 through 12. The denominator is 21 for a six-month contract, 120 for a fifteen-month contract, 171 for an eighteen-month contract, and so on.

[15] Since the "rule of 78" method is so widespread and since it is generally regarded as being fair, no attempt is made here to compare it with the pro-rata method which is also equitable. For such a comparison, see Milan V. Ayres, *Instalment Mathematics*, New York, 1946, pp. 164–170.

is illustrated below by New York's consumer credit laws. (Our use of New York is in no way intended to reflect on the quality of its consumer financing laws. Many other states with consumer financing laws have problems similar to those illustrated here.)

New York's small-loan law specifies computing prepayment refunds by the "rule of 78." The refund would be $68.92 in our example.

Its motor vehicle retail instalment law specifies computing prepayment refunds by the "rule of 78," subject to an acquisition cost deduction of $15 and a provision that any amount under $1 need not be refunded. With this variation, the refund would be $63.56 in our example, i.e., finance charge ($192) less acquisition cost ($15) multiplied by the fraction of months remaining (28/78).

Its retail instalment sales law (excluding autos) specifies computing prepayment refunds by the "rule of 78," subject to a minimum finance charge of $12 on contracts over eight months and $10 on contracts of eight months or less and a provision that any amount under $1 need not be refunded. In our example the prepayment refund would be $68.92 because the finance charge earned through the fifth month exceeded $12. If, however, a creditor has earned less than the specified minimum at the date of prepayment, he can deduct the difference between the minimum and whatever he has earned from the prepayment refund.

Its instalment loan law specifies computing prepayment refunds by the "rule of 78," subject to a minimum finance charge of $10 and a provision that any amount under $1 need not be refunded. This is similar to the retail instalment sales law (excluding autos) and the refund in our example would be $68.92.

Its industrial loan law states that any prepayment refund shall be the unearned portion of the interest previously deducted on an instalment loan. Since no computation method is specified, we cannot work out what the refund would be in an example. The law does not specify any acquisition cost deduction or a minimum finance charge.

These differences in the laws of New York (and those of other states) raise several questions. New York's auto financing law has an acquisition cost deduction but no minimum charge. Its other retail instalment financing law and its instalment loan law have a minimum charge but no acquisition cost deduction. Retail instalment financing laws in most other states have both. To illustrate, the auto instalment financing laws of Florida, Louisiana, and Maine specify minimum charges of $25 *and* acquisition cost deductions of $25. In contrast, many industrial, instalment, and small-loan laws have neither minimum charges nor acquisition cost deductions, and the rest have minimum charges but no acquisition cost deductions.

The purpose of a minimum charge and an acquisition cost deduction is the same, namely, to permit a creditor to cover some or all of the acquisition expenses involved in putting a credit transaction on the books. If they serve the same purpose, the question arises whether the inclusion of both is double counting of acquisition expense.

A second question concerns the level of minimum charges and acquisition cost deductions. Both vary widely within and between state laws which have provisions governing them. Minimum charges and acquisition cost deductions vary from $10 to $25 in automobile financing laws and from $5 to $20 in other retail instalment financing laws. Minimum charges vary from 25 cents to $2 in small-loan laws and from $1 to $15 in industrial and instalment loan laws. Ideally, a minimum charge or acquisition cost deduction should be based on the cost situation of each creditor. This is not practical for legislative purposes due to the inherent difficulties in measuring costs by type of credit.

Table D–1 indicates that twenty-three of the forty-three state supervisors who responded to the State Supervisor Survey were opposed to any acquisition cost deduction on prepaid contracts and thirty-three were opposed on refinanced contracts. It also indicates that most of them favored a uniform method of computing refunds and uniform acquisition deductions for all financing agencies and sellers. The sixteen supervisors who favored an acquisition cost deduction on contracts prepaid in full suggested the following amounts:

	Number of Replies
Amount	
$5	2
$10	3
$10–$15	2
$15	2
$5 on loans to $500; $10 on loans from $501–$1,000; and $15 on loans over $1,000	1
1 per cent with a $1 minimum and a $10 maximum	1
Greater of $2 or 1 per cent of loan	1
Actual cost if prepayment occurs within six months	1
Amount calculated from usual table for refunds	1
Amount determined by each financing agency	1
No reply	1

The amounts in these replies are less than acquisition cost deduction allowances in most existing retail instalment financing laws and are greater than acquisition cost allowances in most existing instalment cash lending laws.

A third question is whether minimum charge and acquisition

TABLE D-1

State Supervisor Survey Replies to Questions
on Prepayment Refunds

Question	Yes	No	Don't Know	No Reply
Should an acquisition cost deduction be allowed in computing the refund on:				
Cash prepayment in full?	16	23[a]	—	4
Refinancing?	3	33	—	7
Should refund method, deduction allowance, and date from which refund is computed be uniform throughout the country for:				
All types of financing agencies and sellers?	35	3	1	4
All types of retail instalment financing?	36	3	1	3
All types of instalment cash loans?	37	3	—	3

[a] Two replies were "no" subject to a nominal minimum charge.

cost deduction provisions should apply both to cash prepayment in full and refinancing or only to the former? As Table D–1 shows, a majority of state supervisors are opposed to both. Only three supervisors say that they favor an acquisition cost deduction on refinancing.

Several factors help explain these results. A creditor loses unearned finance charges on cash prepayment in full. He does not lose unearned finance charges on refinancing, however, since a new (and usually larger) instalment debt replaces a previously existing one. Acquisition cost on refinancing is less than on new financing, and any minimum charge is probably more than covered in the original and refinanced contracts combined. Second, creditors have little incentive to encourage cash prepayment in full and a strong incentive to encourage refinancing. Many financing agencies and sellers actively encourage refinancing through general advertising and through direct contact with existing borrowers.[16] A few laws attempt to discourage early refinancing by specifying that their minimum charge and acquisition cost deduction provisions shall not apply on instalment contracts which are refinanced within four months of the date of the original contract.

A fourth question concerns the date that should be chosen from which to compute the prepayment refund. The relevant possibilities and state supervisor preferences are:

Suggested Date Used in Computing Prepayment Refunds	Distribution of Replies of Supervisors
Date of prepayment	15
Instalment payment date following date of prepayment	13
Instalment payment date preceding date of prepayment	1
Nearest instalment payment date	12
No reply	2
Total	43

All of these possibilities are in existing laws. Table D–1 indicates that thirty-five, or over 80 per cent, of the forty-three supervisors favor a uniform date for all financing agencies and sellers.

A fifth question concerns minimum refund. Most retail instalment financing laws provide that any amount below $1 need not

[16] See *Special Report on Licensed Lenders*, p. 20.

be refunded. Relatively few cash loan laws have a minimum. Those which do specify minimums go up to $3, but for the most part range from 25 cents to $1.

Financing agencies and sellers can make greater refunds than are specified in the law but cannot legally make smaller ones. No data are available on the extent to which financing agencies and sellers make only those refunds required by the laws under which they operate, on the refund practices of financing agencies and sellers whose refund practices are not controlled by law, or on the economic effects of varying refund practices.

Partial Prepayment. A few of the small-loan laws which permit advance charges require lenders to give prepayment refunds when borrowers prepay three or more instalments in full. They generally specify that such refunds shall be computed by the following application of the direct ratio (or "rule of 78") method. The refund which would be due for prepayment in full one month prior to the maturity date should be computed and multiplied by the number of full months the three or more instalments are prepaid. Lenders are permitted to compute and make the refunds at the end of the contract period.

On prepayment of three instalments, this procedure results in one-half of the lowest possible refund that could be obtained by using the application of the "rule of 78" described in the section above on prepayment in full. This can be illustrated by the example on pages 113-114. Under the procedure prescribed in present small-loan laws, the refund for prepayment of three instalment payments would be

$$3 \times \frac{1}{78} \times \$192, \text{ or } \frac{3}{78} \times \$192, \text{ or } \$7.38.$$

Under the procedure for full prepayment, it is necessary to make an assumption about which three instalment payments are to be considered prepaid for purposes of computing the prepayment refund. The lowest refund is obtained by assuming the last three instalment payments are being prepaid. Under this assumption, the refund in our example would be

$$\left(\frac{1}{78} + \frac{2}{78} + \frac{3}{78} \right) \times \$192, \text{ or } \frac{6}{78} \times \$192, \text{ or } \$14.76.$$

This figure is double the previous answer of $7.38. The same relative results obtain in prepayment of three instalments on any contract length because the numerators of the refund fractions for the last three months are always 3, 2, and 1. Analogous differences on prepayments for four, five, and six instalments are as follows:

Number of Instalments Prepaid	Refund Under Full Prepayment Procedure as a Multiple of Refund Under Procedure in Small-Loan Laws (per cent)
4	250
5	300
6	350

Extension (Deferment, Renewal). Data cited in the section on refinancing indicate that refinancing and extension occur frequently in consumer instalment financing. Extension provisions are common in retail instalment financing laws and those small-loan laws which permit advance charges. They are less common in instalment and industrial loan laws.

Existing laws specify one of several general methods of computing extension charges. Under the method which is common in small-loan laws, the extension charge is computed at the rates which pertain to new contracts. Borrowers pay the same finance charge rates for extension as they do for original borrowing. A few laws accomplish essentially the same result by giving financing agencies the option of treating extensions as refinancing subject to the provision that no acquisition cost deduction be permitted in computing the prepayment refund.

Under a second method which is common in retail instalment financing laws, the extension charge is computed at a specified per cent per month rate (usually 1 per cent) on declining balances plus, in some cases, a flat charge, e.g., $5. Under this method the extension charge is not computed in the same way as the original finance charge and may result in a higher or lower effective rate. The use of different methods to compute the original finance charge and the extension charge is due to the fact that the original credit transaction comes under the time-price doctrine but the extension transaction does not. The extension is considered a loan of money and the charge is subject to ceilings in the usury or other relevant cash loan laws of the state rather than to the ceilings specified in the retail instalment financing law.

Under a third method found in a few laws, the extension charge is computed as a flat percentage, e.g., 5 per cent of the amount of the instalment which is being extended. Here, too, the effective extension charge rate may be higher or lower than the effective rate in the original contract.

Since an extension represents the granting of additional credit, some additional finance charge is justified. The first method of determining the charge assumes that a borrower's risk status has not changed between the time of the original borrowing and the extension, for it results in the same finance rate that the borrower would pay if he negotiated an equivalent new loan on the extension date. An effective extension rate above or below the original finance rate implicitly assumes a change in the borrower's credit standing between the time of the original credit and extension credit transactions. A possible additional justification of an effective extension rate below the original finance rate is to reduce the incentive of financing agencies to encourage borrowers to extend their credit contracts.

Delinquency (Default). Most of the retail instalment financing laws, most of the small-loan laws which permit advance charges, and approximately half of the instalment and industrial loan laws set maximum delinquency or default charges. Some of these laws also set grace periods.

The several approaches to setting maximum delinquency charges may be outlined as follows:

1. Most laws set a maximum which is independent of the length of the default period. The usual provision here is to set the maximum at either 5 per cent of the delinquent instalment payment or $5, whichever is smaller. A few laws use other figures such as 4 per cent and $4 and a few use the "rule of 78." Under the latter method, the default charge is equal to the prepayment refund

which would result if prepayment in full were made one month before maturity. This version of the "rule of 78" results in flat percentage rates which vary inversely with the original contract maturity as the following examples show:

Contract Maturity in Months	Fraction for Computing Refund for Prepayment One Month Before Maturity	Percentage Rate
3	1/6	16.67
6	1/21	4.76
12	1/78	1.28
18	1/171	.58
24	1/300	.33

2. Some laws set a maximum which varies with the length of the default period. The rates in these laws range from $\frac{1}{2}$ to 2 per cent a month and are applied either on a daily basis or as a flat rate for stated time segments, e.g., 1 per cent for each twenty days or fraction thereof in the default period. A few laws use step rates, i.e., 50 cents from three to seven days overdue, $1 from eight to twenty-four days overdue and $1.50 over twenty-four days overdue.

Under existing laws, debtors in each state pay different default charges to different creditors. They do so not only because of different ways of determining maximum charges but also because of differences in grace periods. Grace periods vary from one to sixteen days, the most numerous being five and ten days.

Several justifications are given for default charges. One is to recompense the creditor for the loss of interest on his principal during the deliquency period and to recompense him for the extra costs involved in handling delinquent accounts. Another is to discourage debtors from being delinquent. The cost approach would lead to different default charges for different creditors. The discouragement approach would lead to uniform default charges, not because consumers all have the same discouragement level but rather because it is impossible to measure differences in discouragement levels. The two approaches could be combined to set different default charges for different creditors.

In addition to default charges, some laws set maximum attorney fees which creditors may charge debtors on delinquent contracts which are turned over to outside attorneys for collection.

POST-CHARGE LAWS

The per cent per month or post-charge method of computing finance charges is contained in small-loan and credit union laws. Most of these laws permit borrowers to prepay loans in full or in part at any time without penalty charge. A few small-loan laws have minimum finance charges ranging from 25 cents to $2.

Borrowers who prepay or refinance a loan are not entitled to any refund since they have not paid any finance charges in advance. The finance charge stops at the date of prepayment on contracts which are refinanced or prepaid in full.[17] Future finance charges are adjusted downward on contracts which are prepaid in part. They are adjusted to the level which would prevail on a new loan equal to the size of the partially prepaid contract immediately after the prepayment is made.

Credit union and small-loan laws permit extension and default charges, computed on a day-to-day basis for the period of extension or default at the finance rate(s) in the original contract. They usually provide that these "late" charges may not be compounded by being added to the principal owed.

Relation of Legislative Provisions to Finance Charge Computation and Quotation

COMPUTATION

As the discussion has indicated, the method of computing finance charges often affects the size of prepayment refunds as well as the amounts of extension, delinquency, and default charges permitted in state laws. The nature of these relationships is summarized in this section and their pertinence to the issue of finance charge quotation is indicated in the section which follows.

The per cent per month or post-charge method of computing finance charges eliminates the problem of prepayment refunds since charges are not paid in advance. The advance-charge methods of computing finance charges influence the level of prepayment re-

---

[17] The effect of prepayment or refinancing is to lower the effective rate below that which would have obtained if the loan had been paid according to the original schedule.

funds because each refund is determined as a given percentage of the original finance charge. This is true whether the refund formula is the almost universally used direct ratio ("rule of 78") or the rarely used annuity (pro-rata) formula.

The relationship between advance-charge computational methods and refunds means that: (1) the higher the original finance charge, the higher is the prepayment refund at any given prepayment point in the contract; (2) the prepayment refund pattern throughout the life of a contract is independent of the method of computing the finance charge; and (3) for any given method of computing charges, the pattern of refunds at any proportional point in the contract (e.g., at one-third of the maturity) exhibits the same pattern as maturities lengthen as the maturity pattern of the original finance charges. Given these relationships, the discussion of prepayment refunds provides no significant arguments for (or against) uniformity in computing finance charges other than those discussed in Appendix A concerning the effect of maturity on finance charges.

Extension charges are affected directly by the method of computing finance charges in some laws, are indirectly affected in other laws, and are unaffected in still other laws. Default charges are not directly affected by the method of computing finance charges in most laws and are indirectly affected in some laws. Because of these varying relations, uniformity in computing finance charges would not, of itself, lead to a much greater uniformity in computing extension and default charges.

QUOTATION

The purpose of quoting methods of computing prepayment refunds and extension and default charges is to permit borrowers to become aware of the costs of deviating from the scheduled repayment of their indebtedness.

Methods of determining prepayment refunds and extension and default charges have no effect on *ex ante* effective rates or computational equivalents in dollars per hundred. For, as we have indicated in Chapter 4, an *ex ante* rate or computational equivalent is determined before the credit is granted on the assumption the credit will be repaid on schedule.

Methods of determining prepayment refunds and extension and default charges do not affect *ex post* effective rates or computational equivalents on those credit contracts which are paid on schedule but do affect *ex post* those on credit contracts not paid on schedule. In the latter contracts, the lower the prepayment refunds and the higher the extension and default charges, the higher will be the *ex post* effective rates or computational equivalents. The high frequency of refinancing, renewal, and extension provides a means for the lender to advertise a low *ex ante* rate but to obtain a considerably higher *ex post* rate.

More uniform methods of finance charge quotation would simplify information given borrowers. Uniformity would have an effect on prepayment refunds only through its effect on the size of finance charges or if there were a related shift from advance- to post-charge computational methods. It would have an effect on extension and default charges only if it resulted in different computational methods *and* if such charges were based on the computational rate or equivalent. Uniformity in determining prepayment refunds and extension and default charges would have no direct effect upon the issue of the method of finance charge quotation.

Glossary

Actual rate. See Effective rate.

Add-on, annual or monthly. A computational method whereby (1) the finance charge for the instalment credit contract as a whole (F) equals the add-on rate, annual (A) or monthly (M), times the principal amount of credit at the start of the contract (P) times the number of years (N) or months (V) in the credit contract; (2) the finance charge is added to the principal; (3) the credit user receives the principal and pays back the principal plus the finance charge in monthly (or other periodic) instalments.

Add-on plus, annual or monthly. A computational method differing from add-on only in that an investigation or service charge (S) is included in computing the finance charge.

Add-on rate, annual or monthly. The percentage rate, annual (A) or monthly (M), used in comparing the finance charge in the add-on and add-on plus computational methods.

Aggregate rates. See Graduated rates.

Aggregated. A term used interchangeably with Add-on in some instalment loan laws.

Carrying charge. See Finance charge.

Ceiling (rate). The maximum rate which a financing agency or other creditors may legally use in computing a finance charge. Ceiling rates are either specified in consumer financing laws or set by administrative bodies appointed under such laws.

Combination rates. See Graduated rates.

Composite rates. See Graduated rates.

Computational equivalent. The monthly or annual dollar charge per $100 of credit advanced or outstanding used to compute the finance charge. Also expressed as a Computational rate.

Computational rate. The monthly or annual percentage rate used to compute the finance charge. It is applied to the dollar amount either of credit advanced or of credit outstanding. Also expressed as a Computational equivalent.

Credit service charge. See Finance charge.

Discount. A computational method whereby (1) the finance charge for the instalment contract as a whole (F) equals the annual discount rate (D) times the principal amount of credit at the start of the contract (P) times the number of years in the credit contract (N); (2) the finance charge is deducted from the principal; (3) the credit user receives the difference between the principal and the finance charge and pays back the principal in monthly (or other periodic) instalments.

Discount plus. A computational method differing from discount only in that the investigation or service charge (S) is included in computing the finance charge.

Discount rate. The annual percentage rate (D) used in computing the finance charge in the discount and discount plus computational methods.

Effective rate, annual or monthly. The finance charge as a percentage per unit of time (i.e., per month or per annum) of the average unpaid balance of the credit contract during its scheduled life. The counterpart of a bond yield in investment. Also called Actual rate; annual effective rate also called Finance rate.

Finance charge (F). The dollar charge or charges for consumer credit excluding (1) any filing and recording fees which financing agencies and sellers collect from credit users in connection with a credit transaction and (2) any charges on insurance written in connection with a credit transaction. Also called Carrying charge, Credit service charge, Interest charge, and Time-price differential.

Finance rate. See Effective rate, annual.

Flat rate. A single rate used in computing a finance charge.

Graduated rates. Two or more rates used in computing the finance charge on a given loan, each rate being applied to a successive portion of the loan. Also called Aggregate, Combination, Composite, and Multiple rates.

Interest charge. See Finance charge.

Monthly add-on adaptation for revolving credit. An adaptation of the monthly add-on computational method whereby (1) the finance charge for a given month (G) equals the monthly rate applied to loan balances at the beginning of each month (T) times the loan balance at the beginning of each month (W); (2) the finance charge is added to the credit balance; (3) the credit user is expected to pay a portion of that total in that month.

Multiple advance charge. A charge, collected in advance, divided into two or more components, one called interest and the other(s) service charges and fees.

Multiple rates. See Graduated rates.

Multiple effective rates. Separate effective monthly or annual rates on successive portions of a credit contract.

Per cent per month on declining (unpaid) balance. A computational method whereby (1) the finance charge for a given month of the instalment contract (G) equals the monthly rate applied to loan balances at the end of each month (T) times the loan balance at the end of each month (W); (2) since the loan is usually paid off in instalments, G gets smaller each month; (3) the finance charge for the instalment contract as a whole (F) equals G_1 plus G_2 plus G_3 plus . . . G_v. Also called Simple interest method and True interest method.

Precomputation. A computational method whereby (1) the finance charge for the instalment contract as a whole (F) is computed using the method described under (3) of Per cent per month on declining balance (an alternative procedure is described on page 15); (2) the finance charge is added to the principal; (3) the credit user receives the principal and pays back the principal plus the finance charge in monthly (or other periodic) instalments.

Prepayment refunds. Refund of part of the finance charge (F) on credit contracts which the borrower pays in full or refinances before maturity. Such a refund occurs only on credit contracts in which the finance charge is added to or subtracted from the principal at the time the credit is extended.

Revolving credit. A continuing credit arrangement between a seller and buyer in which the buyer (1) agrees to make monthly payments equal to a stipulated percentage of the amount owed at the start of the month plus interest and (2) is permitted to make additional credit purchases as long as the total debt owed does not exceed an agreed-upon limit.

Simple interest method. See Per cent per month on declining balance.

Time-price differential. See Finance charge.

True interest method. See Per cent per month on declining balance.

Index

unions; Industrial banks; Remedial loan societies; Sales finance
companies
Lending, social attitude toward, 9–12,
17–18
Lindsay, S. M., 11n
Liquid assets:
extent of, 56, 58
substitute for debt, 56, 58
use during unemployment, 54, 56
yields, 40–42, 44, 65
See also Consumers; Finance rates
Lorenz, O. C., 21n

Macauley, F., 76n
Maturity, *see* Demand elasticity; Fi-
nance rates
Minnesota Governor's Study Commit-
tee on Consumer Credit, 38, 38n
Monthly payments:
credit cost measure, 40–41
effect on credit demand, *see* Demand
elasticity
Moore, G. H., 112n
Morris, A., 16–18, 17n
Mors, W., 28n
Mott-Smith, H. M., 21n
Multiple effective rates, 33
See also Credit cost measures
Multiple rates, *see* Graduated rates

National Automobile Dealers Associa-
tion, 73–74
National Conference of Commissioners
on Uniform State Laws, 38
National Federation of Remedial Loan
Associations, 12–14
National Recovery Act, 37
Neifeld, M. R., 30n, 63n, 70n, 93, 96n
New York State Banking Department,
32, 110n, 118n
Nugent, R., 11n, 12n, 13n, 28n, 37, 37n

Pawnbrokers, 10
Per cent per month, 28–33
See also Computational method;
Finance rates
Personal loan laws, *see* Instalment loan
laws
Plummer, W. C., 21n, 22n, 23n
Post-charge laws:
definition, 26, 112
legislative provisions, 123

Precomputation, 28–33
See also Computational method
Prepayment refunds:
acquisition cost deduction, 115–116
cash prepayment versus refinancing,
117–118
date for use in computation, 118
legal variations within a state, 114–
119
method of computation:
pro-rata, 113, 114n
rule of 78, 29–30, 113–115, 119–120
minimum, 115–116, 118–119
offsets, 114–115
provisions in advance-charge small-
loan laws, 29–31
relation to finance charge, 123–125
state supervisor attitudes on, 113,
116–118
types, 109, 112–120

Rates, *see* Add-on; Add-on plus; Computational equivalents; Computational rates; Discount; Discount
plus; Effective rates; Finance rates;
Graduated rates; Interest rates; Multiple effective rates; Per cent per
month; Precomputation; Sales finance companies
Recording fees, *see* Filing and recording fees
Redfield, J. M., 28n, 33n
Refinancing, 32–33, 109–111, 113
Regulation W, 46
Remedial loan laws, 18
Remedial loan societies, 10, 12–14, 17n,
18
Renewal, *see* Extension
Retail instalment financing, 20, 24–27,
35–36, 69, 73, 75, 78, 113, 115–118,
120–121
Revolving credit, 27–28
determination of finance rates, 71–
72
laws, 27, 36, 78
monthly add-on adaptation in computing charges, 27–28
Robbins, W. D., 32n
Robinson, L. N., 11n, 12n, 13n, 28n,
110n
Russell Sage Foundation, 12–15, 33, 36,
37n